Focus

Focus

A simplicity manifesto in the Age of Distraction

Leo Babauta

Waking Lion Press

ISBN 978-1-4341-0307-9

Published by Waking Lion Press, an imprint of The Editorium

Waking Lion Press™, the Waking Lion Press logo, and The Editorium™ are trademarks of The Editorium, LLC

The Editorium, LLC
West Valley City, UT 84128-3917
wakinglionpress.com
wakinglion@editorium.com

Contents

Focus: About

About Focus

This book, *Focus,* is by Leo Babauta, creator of zen habits and mnmlist. It was written publicly, online, in small bursts, with feedback from readers throughout the writing process. It would be much worse without their wonderful help.

Dedication

The book is dedicated to my grandfather, Joe Murphy, who lived a life that inspired me, and whose death has left a gap in my life . . . and to my grandmother, Marianne Murphy, whom I love deeply and whose strength and kindness have always pointed the way for me.

Uncopyright

Full Version

The free ebook version of this book can be found at focusmanifesto.com. The full version of the ebook contains additional chapters on:

- creativity and practicing deep focus.
- finding stillness and reflection.
- how to start changes on a broader level.
- overcome the fears that stop you from focusing, by Gail Brenner.
- how to create a minimalist workspace to find focus, by Everett Bogue.
- how to take a digital sabbatical, by Gwen Bell.
- life lessons from tea rituals, by Jesse Jacobs.
- two ways to focus on the stuff that matters, by Michael Bungay Stanier.

In addition, the full version contains video how-to lessons, audio interviews with experts, and bonus guides to help you further learn to focus.

You can get the full version at focusmanifesto.com.

Section I

Step Back

1

Introduction

"Smile, breathe, and go slowly."

–Thich Nhat Hanh

This won't be a long book, a detailed treatise into modern life with an exhaustive system of remedies. It's meant to be short, simple, concise. We'll talk about some of the problems we face as we try to live and create in a world of overwhelming distractions. And we'll look at some simple ways to solve those problems.

And yet, at the heart of this simple book lies the key to many of the struggles we face these days, from being productive and achieving our goals, to getting healthy and fit in the face of fast food and inactivity, to finding simplicity and peace amidst chaos and confusion.

That key is itself simple: focus.

Our ability to focus will allow us to create in ways that perhaps we haven't in years. It'll allow us to slow down and find peace of mind. It'll allow us to simplify and focus on less—on the essential things, the things that matter most.

And in doing so, we'll learn to focus on smaller things. This will transform our relationship with the world. It's not that "less is more," but "less is better." Focusing on smaller things will make us more effective. It'll allow us to do less, and in doing so, have more free

3

time for what's important to us. It'll force us to choose, and in doing so, stop the excesses that have led to our economic problems, individually and as a society.

Focus. Smaller things. Less. Simplicity. These are the concepts that we'll talk about, and that will lead to good things in all parts of our lives.

My Story

If you don't know me, I'm Leo Babauta, best known for my popular blog on simplicity, *Zen Habits,* and my best-selling productivity book, *The Power of Less.*

These concepts of simplicity and focus and less . . . they've been a revelation to me, in my life. In the past few years, I've completely changed my life by changing one thing at a time, by learning to find focus so that I can create, by simplifying and focusing on less.

I thought I'd share this because it's an illustration of how effective these ideas are—and they've worked not only for me but for many of my readers.

By focusing on one thing at a time, small changes, little baby steps, I've been able to change a bunch of habits: I quit smoking, started running, began eating healthier, started waking earlier, and became more organized. And I've accomplished a lot more, taking on one project at a time and using the power of focus and the power of play to accomplish things: running a few marathons and triathlons, simplifying my life, eliminating my debt, starting up a successful blog and business, writing a few books, and much more.

This stuff works. And it's tremendously liberating to discover that you can find focus, you can simplify, and you can change your life.

The Age of Distraction

"Our life is frittered away by detail . . . simplify, simplify."
–Henry David Thoreau

We live in curious times. It's called the Age of Information, but in another light it can be called the Age of Distraction. While humanity has never been free of distraction—from swatting those bothersome gnats around the fireplace to dealing with piles of paper mail and ringing telephones—never have the distractions been so voluminous, so overwhelming, so intense, so persistent as they are now. Ringing phones are one thing, but email notifications, Twitter and Facebook messages, an array of browser tabs open, and mobile devices that are always on and always beeping are quite another. More and more, we are connected, we are up to our necks in the stream of information, we are in the crossfire of the battle for our attention, and we are engaged in a harrying blur of multitasking activity.

When we're working, we have distractions coming from every direction. In front of us is the computer, with email notifications and other notifications of all kinds. Then there's the addicting lure of the browser, which contains not only an endless amount of reading material that can be a black hole into which we never escape, but unlimited opportunities for shopping, for chatting with other people, for gossip and news and lurid photos and so much more. All the while, several new emails have come in, waiting for a quick response. Several programs are open at once, each of them with tasks to complete. Several people would like to chat, dividing our attention even further.

And that's just in front of us. From the sides come a ringing desk phone, a ringing mobile device, music from several different coworkers, a colleague coming to our desk asking a question, incoming papers needing attention, other papers scattered across our desks, someone calling a meeting, another offering up food.

With so much competing for our attention, and so little time to focus on real work, it's a wonder we get anything done at all.

And then we leave work, but the attack on our attention doesn't end. We bring the mobile device, with incoming text and email messages, all needing a reply, with incoming calls that can't be ignored. We have reading material, either in paper form or on the mobile device, to keep our attention occupied. We are bombarded from all sides by advertising, asking for not only attention but our desires. We get home, and there's the television, constantly blaring, with 500 channels all asking for yet more attention, with 500,000 ads asking for yet more desires. There's our home computer, asking us to do more work, sending us more messages, more distractions, social networks and shopping and reading. There are kids or spouses or roommates or friends, there's the home phone, and still the mobile device is going off.

This is unprecedented, and it's alarming.

We've come into this Age without being aware that it was happening, or realizing its consequences. Sure, we knew that the Internet was proliferating, and we were excited about that. We knew that mobile devices were becoming more and more ubiquitous, and maybe some people harrumphed and others welcomed the connectivity. But while the opportunities offered by this online world are a good thing, the constant distractions, the increasingly urgent pull on our attention, the stress of multitasking at an ever-finer granular level, the erosion of our free time and our ability to live with a modicum of peace . . . perhaps we didn't realize how much this would change our lives.

Maybe some did. And maybe many still don't realize it.

I think, with so many things asking for our attention, it's time we paid attention to this.

It's an Addiction

There's instant positive feedback to such constant activities as checking email, surfing the web, checking social networks such as blogs, forums, Twitter and Facebook. That's why it's so easy to become addicted to being connected and distracted.

Other addictive activities, such as doing drugs or eating junk food, have the same kind of instant positive feedback—you do the activity, and right away, you're rewarded with something pleasurable but don't feel the negative consequences until much later. Checking email, or any similar online activity, has that addictive quality of instant positive feedback and delayed negative feedback.

You check your email and hey! A new email from a friend! You get a positive feeling, perhaps a validation of your self-worth, when you receive a new email. It feels good to get a message from someone. And thus the instant positive feedback rewards you checking email, more and more frequently, until the addiction is solidly ingrained.

Now, you might later get tired of answering all your email, because it's overwhelming and difficult to keep up with. But usually by then, you're addicted and can't stop checking. And usually the checking of the email has positive reward (a good feeling) but it's the activity of answering all the emails that isn't as fun.

We'll explore how we can stop this addiction later, in the chapter "the beauty of disconnection."

It's a New Lifestyle

Being connected, getting information all the time, having constant distractions . . . it has all become a part of our lives.

Computers, at one time, were a small part of our lives—perhaps we used them at work, but in the car and on the train, and usually at home and when we're out doing other things, we were disconnected. Even at work, our computers had limited capabilities—we could only do certain things with desktop applications, and while solitaire is definitely addicting, it doesn't take up your entire life.

Not so anymore.

Computers are taking over our lives. And while I'm as pro-technology as the next guy (more so in many cases), I also think we need to consider the consequences of this new lifestyle.

Because we've created a new lifestyle very rapidly, and I'm not sure we're prepared for it. We don't have new strategies for dealing with being connected most of the time, we don't have new cultural norms, nor have we figured out if this is the best way to live life. We've been plunged into it, before we could develop a system for handling it.

It's an Expectation

Let's say you woke up one day and decided you no longer wanted to participate in the Age of Distraction in some way . . . could you just drop out?

Well, you could, but you'd be up against an entire culture that expects you to participate.

A good example was when I recently announced that I was ditching email (more on this later) so that I could focus less on answering emails and more on what I love doing: creating. That seemed fairly straightforward to me, but it turns out it drew quite a strong reaction in a lot of people. Some applauded me for having the courage to give up email—indicating this was a huge step that took bravery, took an ability to break from a major societal norm. Other people were insulted or indignant, either feeling like I was insulting their way of doing things, or that I was some kind of prima donna or "diva" for not wanting to be available through email.

Interesting: the simple act of giving up email was either hugely courageous, or arrogant, because I wasn't living up to the expectation of society that I'd be available via email and at least make the attempt to reply. Interesting, because just a decade earlier, many people didn't use email and no one cared if they didn't.

And email is just one facet of these expectations. How high these expectations are depends on your job, who you are, where you work, and the standards that have evolved in the group you work with. But some people are expected to be available all the time, carrying a Blackberry or other device with them, and to respond almost immediately—or they're out of touch, or not good businesspeople. Others are expected to be available for instant messaging or Skype chats, or be on social forums or social networks such as Facebook or Twitter. Others need to follow the news of their industry closely, and constantly read updates of news sites.

Being connected all the time, being part of this constant stream of distraction, is an expectation that society now has of us. And going against that expectation is immensely difficult for many people—it requires courage, or a willingness to be an arrogant prima donna.

How did this happen? When did we opt-in to be a part of this? There was never a time when we agreed to these expectations, but they've evolved rapidly over the last decade or so, and now it's hard to get out.

I'm not saying we should get out. I'm saying we need to rethink things, to change expectations so that the system suits us, not the other way around.

A Simple Question

Here's a little exercise that might prove useful: as you read this chapter, how many times were you distracted or tempted to switch to another task?

How many times did you think of something you wanted to do, or check your email or other favorite distractions? How many times did you want to switch, but resisted? How many different things made a noise or visual distraction while you were reading? How many people tried to get your attention?

In an ideal world, the answers to all those questions would be "zero"—you'd be able to read with no distractions, and completely focus on your task. Most of us, however, have distractions coming from all sides, and the answers to this little exercise will probably prove illuminating.

3

The Importance of Finding Focus

"Most of what we say and do is not essential. If you can eliminate it, you'll have more time, and more tranquility. Ask yourself at every moment, 'Is this necessary?"

–Marcus Aurelius

If you're someone who creates, in any way, focus should be important to you.

And this includes a much larger group than the traditional "creative types"—artists, writers, photographers, designers, musicians and the like. No, people who create are a much larger group than that, though creative types are included. Those who create include:

- those who invent and create products or services
- teachers who create lessons and activities and content for students professors who write syllabi and lectures
- anyone who writes research papers
- stay-at-home parents who create activities for their kids executives who create plans, presentations, visions, proposals ad execs who create ad campaigns
- bloggers
- people who make websites of any kind
- anyone who writes reports
- someone who crafts physical products like clothing, cars, etc.

- kids who have to do homework
- and many other types of people

In short, it includes most of us, in one way or another.

Focus is crucial to those of us who create, because creating is so difficult without it.

How Distraction Hurts Creativity

It's fairly difficult to create when you're reading a blog or forum or tweeting or sending an email or chatting. In fact, it's almost impossible to do these things and create at the same time.

Sure, you can switch back and forth, so that you're creating and engaging in any of these activities of consuming and communicating. We've all done that.

But how effective is that? When we switch between creating and communicating through email, say, we lose a little bit of our creative time, a little bit of our creative attention, each time we switch. Our mind must switch between modes, and that takes time. As a result, our creative processes are slowed and hurt, just a little, each time we switch.

Here's the catch: creating is a completely separate process from consuming and communicating.

They don't happen at the same time. We can switch between them, but again, we're hurting both processes as we do that.

All the reading and consumption of information we do, all the communicating we do, and all the switching between modes we do—it all takes away from the time we have to create.

We should note that communicating and consuming information aren't necessarily evil to the person who creates: they actually help. We shouldn't throw them out completely. Communicating with others allows us to collaborate, and that actually multiplies our creative power, in my experience. When you communicate and collaborate, you bounce ideas off people, get ideas from things they say, learn from each other, combine ideas in new and exciting ways, build things that couldn't be possible from one person.

When you consume information, you're helping your creativity as well—you find inspiration in what others have done, you get ideas, you gather the raw materials for creating.

But consuming and communicating aren't creating. They aid creating, they lay the groundwork, but at some point we need to actually sit down and create. Or stand up and create. But create.

How to Beat Distraction, and Create

If the problem is that these separate processes of creating, consuming and communicating get in the way of each other, the solution is obvious: we need to separate the processes. We need to create at different times than we consume and communicate.

I know, easier said than done.

But that's what the rest of this book will be about: how to separate these processes. Because in the end, when you separate them, you'll free up your time and mind for creating, and create better and more prodigiously than ever before.

Separate your day: a time for creating, and a time for consuming and communicating. And never the twain shall meet.

You can split your day into many different combinations of the two, but don't put them all together. Or if you do, just be aware that you're hurting your creativity. That's OK sometimes, as there isn't a need to be uber-productive, as long as you're doing something you enjoy. But if your interest is in creating, separate your day.

Focus, Distraction and Happiness

There's more to focus and distraction than just creating, though. Constant connectivity and distractions, and a lack of focus, can affect our peace of mind, our stress levels, and our happiness.

In the days when computers took up only part of our lives, there were times when we could get away from them, when we were disconnected from the grid. Unfortunately, many people still filled much of that time with watching television, which isn't much better.

But it's important to get away from these constant distractions—we need some quiet, some time to reflect and contemplate, some time for solitude. Without it, our minds are constantly bombarded by information and sensations, unable to rest. That constantly stresses our minds in ways we're not meant to handle.

We need the rest. It's important in ways we don't often think about. We need to de-stress, and we need to recharge our mental batteries.

Quiet and solitude and reflection lead to greater happiness when they're a part of our daily lives, at least in some degree. What you do during this time—read, write, run, nap, sit, watch, listen, even have a quiet conversation, play, study, build—isn't as important as the simple fact of having that time of disconnection.

We'll look at how to find this time, and how to find focus, in later chapters. At this point, we just need to note that these things are important.

4

The Beauty of Disconnection

"Without great solitude no serious work is possible."

–Pablo Picasso

There are days when I wake up and refuse to turn on the Internet, and sit still with my cup of coffee in the hush that fills the hours just before dawn. I'll listen to the quiet. I'll reflect on life. I'll lose myself in a novel. Some days I'll sit down and write, just my thoughts and the quiet and the gentle tapping of the keyboard.

And it's beautiful.

Other days I'll go for a run and enjoy the rich outdoor air, salty when I jog by the ocean, sweet when I pass a field of wildflowers, saturated with soft light. And this is a wonderful time for me, as I enjoy the moment, as I soak in the quietness, as I bask in my connection with life but my disconnection with technology.

Other times I'll sit with a friend and have a cup of coffee and chat. We'll argue about politics, or whose computer OS is better, or tease each other, or share stories. While disconnected from technology.

And some days, I take a walk or go for a run with my wife. Or I'll sit with my child, and read, or just play.

These are unbeatable moments.

These are the moments when disconnection shows its glorious face, when life is in full force, when we are fully connected to the world immediately around us, while disconnected from the world at large.

These moments have become increasingly rare and fleeting, because of our connectedness with technology. And that's a sad thing in my book.

I'm no Luddite—I don't think we should abandon technology. It's given me the career and life that I've always wanted, where I'm able to play for a living, create, be a full-time writer, help others, and live a simple life. Technology has empowered me, and I am as big a proponent of the latest technologies as anyone.

It's not technology we should be afraid of. It's a life where we're always connected, always interrupted, always distracted, always bombarded with information and requests. It's a life where we have no time to create, or connect with real people.

Disconnection is the solution, or at least an integral part of it. It's very difficult for many people, because connection is addictive. We'll talk more about that in a minute.

The Benefits of Disconnection

Why should we even consider disconnecting from the grid of information and communication? Let's look at just a few reasons:

• You shut off the interruptions and distractions of email, Twitter, IM, blogs, news, and more.

• You give yourself space to focus and work.

• You allow yourself space to create.

• You can connect with real people without distractions. You can read, you know, books.

• You can accomplish a lot more.

• You allow yourself a break from the stress of overload. You can find quiet and peace of mind.

• You can reflect and contemplate.

There are dozens of other good reasons, but I think those are serviceable for our needs.

How to Disconnect

So how do we go about disconnecting? There are varying strategies, and no one is better than another. I won't be able to tell you what will work best for you—I suggest you experiment, and find a method that fits your needs and situation best. Often that will be a hybrid approach, which is perfectly great—every person is different, and no cookie-cutter approach will work for everyone.

Some ideas:

• *Unplug.* Just unplug your network connector or cable, or turn off your wireless router, or go to your connections settings and disable temporarily. Close your browser and open another program so you can focus on creating without distraction. Do this for as long as you can.

• *Have a disconnect time each day.* It's like setting office hours if you're a professor—you set the times that work best for you, and you can even let people know about these times. Let's say you are disconnected from 8–10 a.m. each day, or 4–5 p.m., or even anytime after 2 p.m. Tell people your policy, so they know you won't be available for email or IM. And use this time to create.

• *Work somewhere without a connection.* For me, this might be the public library—while it has computers with Internet access, there's no wireless in my library. Some coffeeshops don't have wireless connection. Some of you might have to look for a good building that's quiet but doesn't have free wireless. Go to this disconnected zone ready to create, or perhaps just to relax and enjoy the quiet.

• *Get outside.* Leave your devices behind and go for a walk, or a run, or a bike ride. Enjoy nature. Watch a sunset, go to the beach or a lake or river or forest. Take your child or spouse or friend. Recharge your batteries, reflect and contemplate.

• *Leave your mobile device behind, or shut it off.* When you're on the go, you don't always need to be connected. Sure, the iPhone and Android and Blackberry are cool, but they just feed our addictions, they make the problem worse than ever. If you're driving, shut off your device. If you're meeting with someone, turn off the device so you can focus on that person completely. If you're out with your family or friends and not working . . . leave the device at home. You don't need this personal time to be interrupted by work or your impulse to check on things.

  • *Use blocking software.* If you're doing work on the computer, you can use various types of software to shut yourself off from the Internet, or at least from the most distracting portions of it. For example, you can use software to block your web email, Twitter, favorite news sites, favorite blogs, and so on—whatever your worst distractions are, you can block them selectively. Or block all Internet browsing. We'll talk more about software in a later chapter on tools.

  • *Alternate connection and disconnection.* There are any number of variations on this theme, but let's say you disconnected for 20 minutes, then connected for a maximum of 10 minutes, and kept alternating in those intervals. Or you work disconnected for 45 minutes and connect for 15 minutes. You get the idea—it's almost as if the connected period is a reward for doing good, focused work.

  • *Disconnect away from work.* A good policy is to leave your work behind, when you're done with work, and a better policy is to stay disconnected during that time, or work and browsing will creep into the rest of your life. Draw a line in the sand, and say, "After 5 p.m. (or whatever), I won't be connected, I'll focus on my family and my other interests."

How to Beat the Connection Addiction

Being connected is an addiction—and it's one that can be extremely hard to beat. Trust me, I struggle with it myself, all the time.

Like any addiction, connection has very quick positive reinforcements and only long-term negative consequences. When you take drugs or eat junk food, for example, you get instant pleasure but the negative health effects aren't felt until much, much later, when you're already firmly addicted. So you get the positive reinforcement immediately, each time you do the addictive activity such as eating sweets or taking drugs, giving you a pleasure rush and making you want to do the activity again, as soon as possible. You get the positive reinforcement again, and again, and again, in a constant cycle of positive reinforcement, and soon you're addicted.

Connection works the same way. When we check email and get a new message, it's a little bit of validation that we're worthy of someone else's attention—we get a little ego boost, a little pleasure from this. When we check Twitter or our feed reader and see something that grabs our attention, that's a positive reinforcement, a little bit of reward for checking. And so we check again, and again, until we're addicted.

It's not until much later that we feel the consequences, if we even admit them to ourselves. It's months or years later, much after we're addicted, that we realize we're spending all our time online, that our personal lives have been taken over, that we have lost our ability to find quiet and focus, that our creative time and energies have been eroded by these addictions.

So while I can list all kinds of ways to disconnect, if you're addicted even to a small degree, it won't be a small feat to disconnect and stay disconnected.

How do we beat this addiction, then?

The same way you beat any addiction: by breaking the cycle of positive feedback, and by replacing the old habit with a new one.

And while beating addictions is really a subject to be tackled in another book, let's briefly outline some quick strategies you can use to beat this addiction:

• Figure out your triggers. What things trigger your habits? It's usually something you do each day, something that leads directly to your addicted behavior. List these out.

• Find a new, positive habit to replace the old habit for each trigger. For example, with quitting smoking, I needed a new habit for stress relief (running), a new thing to do after meetings (write out my notes), a new thing to do with coffee in the morning (reading), and so on.

• Try changing each trigger, one at a time. So if you go to check your blogs first thing in the morning, make it a new habit to not open your browser, and instead open a simple text editor and start writing.

• Create positive feedback for the new habit. If the new habit is something you don't enjoy, you'll quit before long. But if it's something enjoyable, that gives you positive feedback, that's good. Praise from others is also a good positive feedback—there are many, and you'll want to engineer your habit change so that you get almost instant positive feedback.

• Create instant negative feedback for the old habit. Instead of having negative feedback be long-term for going online, you want some negative feedback instantly: make it a rule that you have to call someone and tell them you failed if you go online after a certain trigger, for example. There are lots of kinds of negative feedback—maybe you'll have to log and blog your failures, or something like that.

• Repeat the positive feedback cycle as often as possible for the new habit. Soon, after a few weeks, it'll become a new habit and the old one will be (mostly) licked. Repeat for the next trigger.

Starting small, with just one trigger at a time, is a good way to be successful.

5

Focus Rituals

"My only ritual is to just sit down and write, write every day."

–Augusten Burroughs

Focus and creating are about more than just disconnecting. You can be connected and focus too, if you get into the habit of blocking out everything else and bringing your focus back to what's important.

One of the best ways of doing that is with what I like to call "Focus Rituals."

A ritual is a set of actions you repeat habitually—you might have a pre-bed ritual or a religious ritual or a just-started-up-my-computer ritual. One of the powerful things about rituals is that we often give them a special importance: they can be almost spiritual (and sometimes actually spiritual, depending on the ritual). And when they become special, we are more mindful of them—we don't just rush through them mindlessly.

Mindfully observing a ritual is important, especially when it comes to focus, because often we get distracted without realizing it. The distractions work because we're not paying attention. So when we pay attention to a ritual, it's much more conducive to focus, and then to creativity. Mindful attention to a ritual also helps keep it from become too rote or meaningless.

It's important to give importance to each ritual, so that you'll truly allow yourself to focus and not forget about the ritual when it's not convenient. For example, you might start each ritual with a couple of cleansing breaths, to bring yourself to the present, to clear your head of thoughts of other things, and to fully focus on the ritual itself.

Let's take a look at just a few Focus Rituals. Please note that this isn't meant to be a comprehensive list, nor am I suggesting you do all of these. It's a list of ideas—you should try ones that seem best suited for your situation, and test them out to see what works best.

• *Morning quiet.* You start your day in quiet, before the busy-ness of the world intrudes on your peace of mind. If you live with others, you might want to wake before they do. The key to enjoying this focus ritual is not going online. You can turn on the computer if you just want to write. You can have coffee or tea and read. You can meditate or do yoga or do a workout or go for a run. Or take a walk. Or sit quietly and do nothing. The key is to take advantage of this peaceful time to rest your mind and focus, however you like.

• *Start of day.* Begin your work day by not checking email or any other distractions, but start a simple to-do list on paper or with a text file. On this blank to-do list, just list your three Most Important Tasks. Or if you like, just list the One Thing you really want to accomplish today. This helps you to focus on what's important. Even better: continue this focus ritual by starting immediately on the top task on this short list of Most Important Tasks. Single-task on this important task as long as you can—ideally until it's done. Now you've started your day with focus, and you've already accomplished something great.

• *Refocus ritual.* While the start of day ritual is great, there are lots of things that get in the way to distract you, to mess up your focus. So every hour or two, do a refocus ritual. This only takes a minute or two. You might start it by closing down your browser and maybe other open applications, and maybe even take a walk for a couple of minutes to clear your head and get your blood circulating. Then return to your list of Most Important Tasks and figure out what you need to accomplish next. Before you check email again or go back online, work on that important task for as long as you can. Repeat this refocus ritual throughout the day, to bring yourself back. It's also nice to take some nice deep breaths to focus yourself back on the present.

• *Alternate focus and rest.* This is almost like intervals in exercise—alternating between periods of hard exercise and rest works well because it allows you to do some pretty intense exercise, as long as you allow yourself some rest. Focus works much the same way—if you give yourself built-in periods of rest, you can get some great periods of focus. There are many variations on this, but some ideas might include: 10 minutes of focus + 2 minutes of rest; 25 minutes of focus + 5 minutes of rest; 45 minutes of focus + 15 minutes of rest. You get the idea—you'll need to experiment to find the length and mixture that works best for you. Some prefer short bursts and others like longer periods of undisturbed creativity.

• *Alternate two focuses.* Instead of alternating between focus and rest, you could alternate between two different focuses. For example, you could work on two different projects at once, or study for two different classes at once. I'd suggest not switching too rapidly, because there's a short period of adjustment each time you switch. But you could work for 10 minutes on one thing and then 10 on another, or stay focused on one as long as you are interested in it, then switch when your interest lags. The great thing about this method is that switching to a new project can help give your brain a rest from the other project, and it can keep you creating for much longer before getting distracted.

• *Communicate first, then use blocks of focus.* Set a timer and give yourself 45 minutes to do email, Twitter, Facebook IM, and any reading you would normally do. Then use an Internet blocker to block these distractions for a couple of hours (up to 3–4 hours if you like) while you focus on creating. Then another 45 minutes of communicating and reading, followed by another block of distraction-free focus.

• *End of day.* At the end of each day, you might review what you did, think of what can be improved, remind yourself to disconnect for the rest of the evening, and think about what you'll focus on tomorrow. It's a good time to reflect on your day and your life in general.

• *Weekly focus rituals.* While it's not necessary to do a complete weekly review of everything you're doing, have done and plan to do, it can be useful to schedule 10 minutes every week to quickly bring your work and life back into the right focus. I suggest you review your projects to make sure you're not letting them get out of hand; simplify your to-do list as much as possible; review the focus rituals you've been doing to see what's working and what isn't; and basically reflect on what you're doing with work and life and whether anything needs to change.

• *Other ideas.* The rituals above are just some of the ideas I like best—you should find the ritual that works best for you. There are an almost infinite number of possibilities. Just a few other ideas: taking 5 minutes every hour to refocus yourself; taking a walk every hour to get fresh air and get refreshed; yoga or meditating at the beginning of each day; running or other exercise after work; giving yourself a "focus and disconnected hour" in the morning and afternoon where you're disconnected and completely focused on creating; breathing and self-massage techniques for relaxation and better focus.

Section II

Clear Distractions

6

Limiting the Stream

"Time is but the stream I go a-fishing in."

–Henry David Thoreau

The stream of news, information, and messages we get these days is enough to drown us. It's staggering in its volume. It's a wonder anyone can find any focus with an information stream like that.

The Stream of Distractions

The more connected a person becomes on the Internet, the more distractions they face in their day. Just a couple decades ago, most people's distractions consisted of the phone, the fax machine, incoming memos and paperwork, solitaire, and actual people in their offices.

These days, people who work online face much more than that:
- email (perhaps the biggest problem for most people)
- instant messaging Twitter
- Facebook
- online forums
- blogs
- other social networks
- news sites
- phones & cell phones

- text messages
- Skype
- podcasts
- Google alerts
- mobile device notifications (iPhone, Blackberry, etc.)
- mobile apps videos
- online music online shopping Internet radio paperwork
- online games
- solitaire
- internet TV
- ebooks

And more.

Why and How to Limit the Stream

With so many distractions, it's impossible to truly focus on the important. We try to drink the stream, but it's too voluminous and never-ending to take in this way.

Some people think this is just a part of their work, or their lives, and that there's nothing wrong with being connected. It's a part of doing business, they say.

However, there's no one way to do business, and this book is about finding a better way. A saner way. I'm just one example of many people who have managed to do business online, have managed to stay connected, but who are able to limit the stream and make conscious decisions about how to be connected and how much information we consume.

We do it consciously, with intent. Social networks, blogs and news sites you read, different ways to communicate and consume information . . . these tend to build up as you spend time online. You build them up without much thought, but you end up being consumed by what you consume.

I suggest becoming more conscious of this, and choosing what you consume and how much you communicate carefully. Limit your stream to only the most essential information and communications, and you'll free up hours of time for creating and doing amazing things.

I also suggest starting from scratch. Assume that nothing is sacred, empty your plate, and only put back on it what you absolutely need or love. Let the rest fade away.

Make an Important Admission

It's crucial that you admit to yourself: you can't read and consume everything. You can't do everything, respond to everything. Not only would the attempt take up all of your waking hours, but you'd fail. There's too much out there to read, too many people to potentially connect with and respond to, too many possible projects and tasks to actually complete.

It's impossible. Once you admit this, the next logical argument is that if you can't do and read and respond to everything, you must choose what you'll do and read and respond to, and let the rest go.

Let the rest go. This is unbelievably important. You have to accept this, and be OK with it.

An Information Cleanse

If you look at information and communication as a form of mild (or sometimes not-so-mild) addiction, it can be healthy to force yourself to take a break from it.

Go on a mini-cleanse. Start with something that's not so scary: perhaps a day, or even half a day. Do this once a week. Later, as you get used to this, try a 2–3 day cleanse, and maybe even work your way up to a week.

Here's how to do the cleanse:
- Don't check email or other types of digital inboxes.
- Don't log into Twitter, Facebook, or other social networks or forums.
- Don't read news, blogs, subscriptions.
- Don't check your favorite websites for updates.

- Don't watch TV.
- Don't use instant messaging of any kind.
- Do use phones for as little time as possible, only for essential calls.
- Do send an email if necessary, but try to avoid it, and don't check your inbox if you do.
- Do use the Internet for absolutely necessary research. Be vigorous about this rule.
- Do spend your time creating, working on important projects, getting outside, communicating with people in person, collaborating, exercising.
- Do read: books, long-form articles or essays you've been wanting to read but haven't had the time for.
- Do watch informative or thought-provoking films, but not mindless popular movies.

You could make a personalized list of your dos and don'ts, but you get the general idea. Again, start with half a day or a day—something manageable. Do it once a week, and gradually expand the time you spend on the cleanse.

Reducing the Stream

If you've done the cleanse, you now know the value of disconnecting, and you know that you can live without having to check your streams of information and messages all day, every day.

You've cleaned your plate. Now it's time to figure out what to add back on it.

Give it some thought: what are the most essential ways you communicate? Email? Skype? Twitter? Cell phone? IM?

What are the most essential information streams you consume? What blogs? What news? What other reading or watching or listening?

What can you cut out? Can you cut half of the things you read and watch? More?

Try eliminating at least one thing each day: a blog you read, an email newsletter you receive, a communication channel you don't need anymore, a news site you check often. Take them out of your email or feed inbox, or block them using one of the blocking tools mentioned in the "Focus Tools" chapter.

Slowly reduce your stream, leaving only the essentials.

Using the Stream Wisely

Just as importantly, reduce the time you spend using the essentials. If email is essential, do you need to be notified of every new email right this second? Do you need to be in your inbox all day long?

Place limits on the time you spend reading and communicating—a small limit for each channel. Only check email for 30 minutes, twice a day, for example (or whatever limits work for you). Only read the limited number of blogs you subscribe to for 30 minutes a day. Only watch an hour of TV a day (for example).

Write these limits down, and add them up for a grand total of what you plan to spend on reading, consuming, communicating. Is this an ideal amount, given the amount of time you have available to you each day? The smaller the overall limit, the better.

7

You Don't Need to Respond

"Nature does not hurry, yet everything is accomplished."

–Lao Tzu

We have developed a fairly urgent need to respond to many things: mails, Tweets & other social network status updates, instant messages, phone calls, text messages, blog posts, blog comments, forum posts, and more. This need to respond gives us anxiety until we've responded, but unfortunately, there is a never-ending stream of things that require your response.

If we allow these messages to force us to respond, almost as soon as they come, then we become driven by the need to respond. Our day becomes responsive rather than driven by conscious choices. We fit from one task to another, one response to another, living a life driven by the needs of others, instead of what we need, what we feel is important.

You don't need to respond.

Think about why we feel we need to respond to everything. Often it's just a compulsion—we're so used to answering messages that we have developed an urge to respond. Often it's also out of fear: fear that people won't think we're doing our job, fear that we'll lose customers, fear that we'll miss out on something important, fear that people will think we're rude or ignoring them.

But what if we weaned ourselves from this compulsion? And what if we addressed these fears?

1. *First, imagine that you're free from the compulsion.* What would it be like? You'd choose what you're going to do today, and work on the important things. You could still respond to emails and other things, but it would be because you decided it was important to communicate something, not because someone else sent you a message and you felt compelled to reply. You'd be much less stressed out, because you don't feel like you need to get through these piles of things to respond to, or worry about people trying to contact you through various channels.

2. *Next, address the fears.* Think about what specific fears you have—are you afraid people will think you're rude? Are you afraid you'll miss something? Are you afraid you'll lose customers, or get in trouble at work? Figure out what your fears are—there are probably more than one. Now address them with a tiny test—go without responding, just for a few hours. What happened? Did you lose anything? Did you miss anything? Did someone get offended? If nothing bad happens, extend this test—try half a day, or a full day. See what happens. In most cases, nothing bad will happen at all. In a few cases, something negative might happen, but it'll be pretty minor. You'll realize that your fears are mostly ungrounded.

3. *Finally, start weaning yourself.* If you agree that being free of these compulsions would be a better way of living, start moving towards this life. Again, try just a small test—a couple hours every day when you don't respond to things. Set a time, after this "response-free" block of your day, when you do respond. This way, you're in control—you decide when to respond. Eventually, you might increase your "response-free" zone to half a day or more, but start small.

8

Let Go of the Need to Stay Updated

"Fear makes the wolf bigger than he is."

–German proverb

Many of us are slaves to the news, to the need to keep updated with what's happening in the world, in our business niche, with our friends.

We are information junkies in some way: we watch TV news all the time, or entertainment news, or keep up with lots of blogs, or our RSS feed reader, or Twitter, or Digg or Delicious, or email, or one of the many news aggregator sites.

The need to keep up consumes much of our day, and creates a kind of anxiety our minds barely register.

What is this need based on? Why can't we get free of it?

Actually, we can get free. I've done it in my life, to a large extent. Let's examine the two questions.

What Is This Need Based On?

In short: fear.

If we really think about it, we're not gaining much by keeping up with all this information. How is it adding to our lives? How is it helping us to create, to live happy lives, to do what's most important to us, to spend time with our loved ones? If anything, it takes away from these things.

Let me repeat that point: this obsession with keeping up with information takes away from the things that are most important to us.

But we try to keep up because we're afraid:

- We might miss something important, and seem ignorant.
- We might miss out on an opportunity.
- We might not see something bad that we need to respond to.
- Something bad might happen to us if we aren't informed.

These fears seem reasonable, until we test them. Then we can see that they're not really grounded in anything other than societal norms, and a "need" created by media corporations and similar companies.

How to Break Free

There are two ways to break free: 1) examine each fear individually, and 2) test them.

When we shine a light on our fears, they lose power. When we test them to see their validity, they will usually fail, and we can overcome them.

Let's shine a brief light:

- *We might seem ignorant.* Really? How often do people quiz you on current events, or laugh at you for not knowing? Maybe sometimes, but even if it does happen, so what? Let others be fueled by this need, and let yourself focus on things you care about, not what others think is important.

- *We might miss out on an opportunity.* Possibly. There are always going to be opportunities we miss. But more likely are the opportunities we're missing because we're letting our days be consumed by trying to stay up to date. When we do this, we lose time we could be using to pursue exciting, real opportunities.

- *We might not see something bad that we need to respond to.* If something really bad is happening, we'll know. I hear things on

Twitter, even if I only pop in once in a while, and friends and family will always tell me about a storm or economic collapse or something similar. Sure, this is relying on others, but if they're going to tell us anyway, why worry about keeping up ourselves?

• *Something bad might happen to us if we aren't informed.* This is highly unlikely. I've been uninformed—tuned out from the news and other information I don't want—for a few years now. Nothing bad has happened to me. Instead, good things have happened because I'm free to create, to focus on what makes me happy.

The next step is to actually test the fears. Do this by tuning out of the news or whatever information you try to keep up with, for one day. Then see if any of your fears came true.

If not, feel free to read the news you want, peruse the websites you follow. Then try a second test of two days—see what happens. Keep repeating this, but extending the test, until you can go a couple weeks without staying up to date. Then see if your fears are true.

Testing will show you facts. You'll see if something bad happens, or if you appear ignorant, or if you miss out on big opportunities. You'll also see whether you are freer to live the life you want.

9

How Not to Live in Your Inbox

"It's not enough to be busy, so are the ants. The question is, what are we busy about?"

–Henry David Thoreau

Many of us do this—we have our email inbox open most of the day, and most of the time, our work is right there, in the inbox. It's where we live, communicate, keep track of tasks, do our work, organize ourselves.

Unfortunately, it's not the best way to live and work. You're constantly getting interrupted by new messages, and so we're at the mercy of the requests of others. A new email comes in, and so we must stop what we're doing to check the new email, and possibly respond. Even if we don't respond right away, whatever we were just doing was interrupted.

This is the opposite of focus, and nothing exemplifies the need for focus better. Sure, you're always in touch, always up to date, always on top of things. But you have no focus, and you're buffeted in all directions by the winds of your email (or Twitter, Facebook, IM or other communication channels). It's also hard to prioritize when you're living in a sea of emails—every new email become important, and that makes choosing our tasks carefully an almost impossible task.

Here are some suggestions:

• *Get your task list out of your inbox.* An email inbox is a bad to-do list, because it can't be prioritized, emails can't be renamed to reflect the tasks within them, emails have multiple tasks within them, and there are always new emails coming in. Instead, choose a simple to-do list and as you process your email inbox, pull out the actions to the to-do list. A notebook or index card works fine, as does a simple program such as Taskpaper or Things, or even a text file in Notepad or TextEdit or Notational Velocity. If you set up a keyboard shortcut for your to-do app or file, it just takes a second to copy and paste a to-do from an email.

• *Do email only at pre-appointed times.* You'll need to experiment to find the schedule that works best for you, but try to stick to it rather than constantly checking your inbox. Examples might be: check email 5 minutes at the top of each hour, or just twice a day (say, at 9 am and 3 pm), or once a day at 10 am, or twice a week. Again, these are just examples—your needs will dictate the best schedule for you, though I would suggest trying a less frequent schedule than you think you need and seeing if that works.

• *Do your work with your email closed.* When it's not a pre-appointed time to check email, have it closed. This principle, by the way, also applied to any other forms of communication, such as Twitter, Facebook, IM, forums, etc., as well as other distractions such as games. Close them all when you're going to work. In fact, close your browser or at least all the browser tabs you don't need for that specific task. Now work without distraction for at least a short period.

• *Choose your tasks wisely.* Once you're out of your inbox, you can prioritize. You can decide what's important, because you're no longer at the mercy of the requests of others. What's the best use of your time? What tasks will have the most impact on your life and work, rather than just seeming urgent right now?

10

The Value of Distraction

"Don't underestimate the value of Doing Nothing, of just going along, listening to all the things you can't hear, and not bothering."

–A. A. Milne

Reading this book, you might get the idea that distractions are evil and at we must strive to be focused at all times. Not at all. Distraction is natural, it's fun, and interestingly, it's valuable.

Distraction, in most cases, is the enemy of focus, and so if we want to get anything done, we must learn to find at least a modicum of focus, some of the time. But that's not to say we should banish distraction, every minute of the day. What's needed is balance.

Distraction is important for a few reasons:

• Our minds need a break—being focused for long periods of time is stressful and we need to alternate focus with periods of relaxation.

• Distraction can take our minds off a troubling problem, and that can often lead to our minds working on the problem in the background, in our subconscious.

• Distraction can lead to inspiration—by reading other things, new ideas can be sparked, or we can find motivation.

• Distraction is fun. And in fun, we often find things we truly love. Let yourself be open to these new paths.

• Distraction can lead to better focus, once we go back to focusing.

So how can we incorporate healthy distractions, but still find necessary focus? The secret is balance: conscious, purposeful balance.

There are lots of ways to find balance. The key is to think about what you need to focus on, when your peak focusing hours are, and try different styles to find a method that works best for you.

Some ideas:

• Block off a few hours a day (all at once or broken into 2–3 parts) for focus. Let yourself do email and other communicating during the others parts of your day.

• Work in intervals. Focus for 10–15 minutes, then do 2–5 minutes of distraction, and repeat.

• Try a 40–20 split for every hour: 40 minutes of focus, 20 minutes of distraction.

• Disconnect completely for large parts of your day, and have certain periods just for distraction.

Again, these are just some ideas. You'll have to find the method that works best for your work needs and personality.

11

Why Letting Go Can Be Difficult

While it might seem appealing to give up distractions and let go of the addiction to information, email or news, it's not always easy. It's definitely easier said than done.

It's similar to the problem of letting go of possessions—often we have sentimental or emotional attachment to possessions, or worry that we'll need them later or be less secure without the possessions. Clearing out clutter isn't always easy, because of these emotional hurdles.

Letting go of addictions to information and distractions is just as hard. We might want to let go, but when the rubber meets the road, we balk. We have urges. We falter and fall and fail.

Why is that? And how can we overcome these hurdles?

Let's take a look at the biggest difficulties and some ideas for beating them.

• *Addiction.* Information, news and distractions can become an addiction, as we discussed in previous chapters. And beating addictions isn't easy. Even when our motivation to beat the addiction is strong, the urges we feel and rationalizations we make to ourselves can be even stronger.

How do we beat this addiction? We talked about this previously, but in a nutshell, we must beat them individually (not a whole bunch of addictions at once), figure out what our triggers are for that addiction (when do we automatically do the addiction and feel the urges), and become mindful of the triggers and our urges.

Remember that urges are only temporary. If you are aware that you're feeling an urge, you can ride it like a wave—it'll surge and get stronger, and then fade away. Take some deep breaths, and replace the habit with another habit—like doing pushups, going for a walk, or finding a quiet spot and reflecting. If you enjoy the new habit, you can more easily replace the old habit. Ride the urges and you can beat them, one at a time. Eventually the urges will go away and you'll have a new habit that's more conducive to focus.

• *Filling an emotional need.* Each distraction fills a need in some way. You do the distraction for a reason. New email gives you a little feeling of satisfaction, a confirmation that you're important. So do new replies on Twitter or Facebook or other online forums, or text messages or phone calls. Entertaining distractions fill a need to avoid boredom, or a need to rest from work that strains our mind. There are other similar emotional needs that these distractions fill, but the key is to consider each need.

What happens when we try to remove these distractions? We feel a void where they used to be. Which means we need to find a way to fill that void.

If you get satisfaction or a feeling of importance from new emails or other notifications or messages . . . it's important to be honest with yourself about that. Why do these interruptions, notifications, make you feel good? Is there another way to get validation? Maybe it's good to find recognition instead from the accomplishments and creations that result from finding focus.

If you try to avoid boredom, perhaps it's important to find things that excite you, that you're passionate about. Someone pursuing a passion doesn't need solitaire or Farmville to avoid boredom.

Whatever the emotional need, be honest about it, be conscious of it, and find other ways to fulfill it.

• *Fears.* As we discussed earlier, often we feel the need to stay up-to-date, with news or by checking email constantly or other similar ways of staying in touch. We fear being out of touch, being uninformed.

The only way to beat fears is to face them, and confront them with facts.

Fears have the most power when we don't confront them, when we let them hide in the dark and exercise their quiet influence over our lives. So the key to beating these fears is to face them. Be honest—what are you afraid of?

Then shine a light on these fears with actual facts—what harm has actually been caused so far? Try to do a short test—an hour, a day, a few days, a week—and see what the results are. In most cases the actual harm will be much less than you fear. For example, try going a day without responding to email—see whether you missed anything that was truly important. By getting actual results, the fears will be shown to be baseless (in most cases, I'd guess).

More on beating fears later, in the chapter by psychologist Gail Brenner.

• *Desires.* Sometimes we have trouble letting go of these addictions because of desires—the desire to be successful at something, for example, or the desire to be seen as good at something, or the desire to build wealth.

If we have a strong desire to be a successful blogger or Internet marketer, to take just two examples, we might try to connect with as many other bloggers or readers or marketers as possible, and try to attract as many followers as possible on Twitter and our blog, all of which would require lots of time emailing, tweeting, blogging, commenting on blogs, and so forth.

If the desire wasn't there, the need to connect all the time wouldn't be there. Now, I can't say whether you want to get rid of the desire, but it's important to be honest about what your desires are, what the consequences are when it comes to these addictions, and whether that's how you want to live your life. If you're OK with these desires and their consequences, at least you're aware of them.

If you want to drop the desire, it's not simple, but it can be done. I'd suggest first thinking about why you want to drop the desire—because of negative consequences—and then be more aware when the desire comes up at different times during the day. Just like addictive urges, desires will come and go, and taking some deep breaths and riding out the desire will help you get through it. Eventually, you'll learn that you don't need the desire.

12

Tools for Beating Distraction

"Man must shape his tools lest they shape him."

–Arthur Miller

This is a resource for those who need a little help in blocking out distractions. It's software that will block websites and other time-wasters, or clear away everything on your computer but what you need to focus on.

It's important to note, however, that these types of software are not a solution, but tools to aid your new habits of focus. It's best to learn new habits of simplifying, clearing distractions, staying mindful of the task you're working on. These tools can help you get started, but they're not absolutely necessary, and if you do use them at first you might find you don't need them forever.

Mac

Freedom—An extreme tool, but an effective one. Disables your entire Internet connection for a time period set by you. Perfect when you really need to focus for an hour or three at a time.

Self-control—Disable access to mail servers and websites that distract you. For example, you could block access to Facebook, Gmail, Twitter, and your favorite blogs for 90 minutes, but still have access to the rest of the web. Once started, you can't undo it until the timer runs out.

Concentrate—Create an activity (design, study, write, etc.) and choose actions (launch or block websites, quit applications, speak a message, and more) to run every time you concentrate. When ready, just click "concentrate." All your distractions will disappear and a timer will appear to help you stay focused.

WriteRoom—Perhaps the first, and still one of the absolute best, distraction-free text editors. Goes full screen so all you have is your text. No formatting, no nothing—just writing text. Beautiful program, copied by many others.

Ommwriter—Beautiful app just for writing. Has a serene backdrop with background music, perfect for creating the distraction-free writing environment (especially if you use headphones). Can adjust some of the settings but most of the time, it's just your text, your Zen-like background, and the music.

Ulysses or Scrivener—Two great programs for writers, many more features than WriteRoom but great for longer works such as novels, screenplays, academic papers and more. Both feature full-screen text editors.

Megazoomer—A cool little app that allows you to put almost any Mac program into full-screen mode (à la WriteRoom) using a system-wide keyboard command or menu item. Requires you to install SIMBL—both programs are free.

Think—Little utility that will fade out everything but the app you're working on at the moment. Allows you to focus on one document at a time, clearing the distractions.

Browser Plugins/Extensions

LeechBlock (Firefox)—Specify what sites you want to block in Firefox, and when to block them.

StayFocusd (Chrome)—Choose certain sites to block, and you get 10 minutes total (by default) per day to go on those time-wasting sites. You can change the time allotted for time-wasting sites, and you can also "nuke" (block) all sites for a time you specify.

Readability (bookmarklet, Chrome extension)—clears the clutter on any web article or blog post you want to read. Removes everything—ads, icons, widgets, and more—and just leaves the content in a nice, uncluttered, readable design. Quietube does the same for videos.

Windows

Dark Room—WriteRoom clone for Windows.

CreaWriter—Distraction-free writing tool inspired by OmmWriter (above), with a peaceful background, full-screen writing, soothing ambient sound, and not much else.

Q10—Full-screen text editor with a timer for focused writing, typewriter sounds as you type if you want them. Freeware.

WriteMonkey—new entry into the full-screen editor field. In the words of the makers: "Zenware for full screen distraction free creative writing. No whistles and bells, just empty screen, you and your words. WriteMonkey is light, fast, and perfectly handy for those who enjoy the simplicity of a typewriter but live in modern times."

Other

Emacs—One of the classic text editors (vim is a good alternative and we won't into which is better here), Emacs runs on all platforms (PC, Mac, Linux) and can hid the menu bar (M-x menu-bar-mode) and tool bar (M-x tool-bar-mode) in any operating system, and can hide also the window title bar in most Linux window managers.

Typewriter—A minimalist text editor that runs in Java (which can run on most operating systems—Mac, Windows, Linux). All you can do is type in one direction. You can't delete, you can't copy, you can't paste. You can save and print. And you can switch between black text on white and green on black; full screen and window. Perfect for writing without stopping, and getting out that first draft.

Section III

Simplify

13

Creating an Uncluttered Environment

"If your mind isn't clouded by unnecessary things, then this is the best season of your life."

–Wu-Men

Imagine you're trying to create your masterpiece—a work that will change your life and perhaps make the world a better place in some small way. You're at your computer, making it happen, at a desk piled with clutter, surrounded by clutter on the floor and walls, in the middle of a noisy workplace, phones ringing. A notification pops up—you have a new email—so you open your email program to read it and respond. You get back to work but then another notification pops up—someone wants to chat with you, so you go on IM for a little bit. Then your Twitter client notifies you of some new replies, and you check those. Then you see some paperwork on your desk you need to file, so you start doing those.

But what happened to your masterpiece? It never gets done in a cluttered, scattered workspace like this.

Now imagine a different workspace: a clear desk, with only a couple of essential items on it. A clear computer desktop, with no icons to distract you. There's nothing on the floor around you, and very little on the walls. You have some nice ambient music to block out surrounding noise (perhaps using headphones), and there are no notifications that pop up to interrupt you. All you have on your computer is one open program with one open window, ready to work on your masterpiece.

The difference is striking, and it illustrates the importance of an uncluttered workspace with few interruptions, when it comes to focusing.

This is true not only of an office workspace, but of anywhere you want to focus: at home, outside, at a coffee shop where you want to do some work. The less clutter and distractions you have, the better you'll be able to focus.

How to Get Started

It's important to remember that you don't need to create the perfect uncluttered environment right away. If you do it all in one go, you could spend hours or even all day working on this project, and then you'll have gotten nothing done.

My suggestion is to work in small chunks. Just 10–15 minute improvements once or twice a day, and slowly you'll be creating a wonderful environment. But you'll see improvements immediately.

For example, you might do 10–15 minutes at a time, working in this order:

1. Clear your desk.
2. Turn off computer notifications.
3. Find soothing music and some headphones.
4. Clear your computer desktop.
5. Clear your floor.
6. Clear your walls.

And so on, improving one area at a time. Once you have things pretty clear, don't worry about tweaking things too much. Creating the "perfect" environment can become just as much a time-waster and distraction as anything else.

You could also do all those things at once if you really want to, and have the time. I don't recommend it, but I've done it myself in the past, so I understand this urge.

Let's look at how to do all of the above things as simply as possible.

Start with Your Desk

We're going to focus just on the top of your desk. You can sort through the drawers another time.

First, take a quick survey—what do you have on top of your desk? Papers, folders, binders? A computer, printer, fax machine, phone, stapler, file tray? Post-it notes, phone messages and other scraps of paper? Coffee cup, food, water bottle? Photos, mementos, trinkets, plaques? What else?

Now make a very short mental list: what on your desk is absolutely essential? Just pick 5 items, perhaps. Maybe something like this: computer, phone, water bottle, photo of loved one, inbox tray. Your list will probably be different.

Now take everything off the desk except those items. Put them on the floor. Wipe off your desk with a sponge or rag, so you have a nice clean desk, and arrange the few items you have left nicely. Isn't that lovely?

If you have time, deal with the items you put on the floor now. If not, stack them somewhere out of the way and deal with them the next time you have 10–15 minutes.

Here's what to do with them: pick up one item from the group, and make a quick decision: do you need it, or can you get rid of it or give it to someone else? If you need it, find a place for it that's not on top of your desk—preferably out of sight in a drawer. Always keep it there if you're not using it at the moment.

If you don't need it, give it to someone else or recycle/trash it. Work through all your items quickly—it should only take 10–15 minutes to do this. If you have a bunch of files/papers that need to be sorted or filed, worry about those later. Put them in a to-be-filed drawer, and file them when you get your next 10–15 minute chunk.

From now on, you'll only have things on top of the desk that you're going to use at this moment. If you're not using the stapler, put it away. If you're not working on that file, file it. You could have a "working folder" and put files/papers in there that you're going to use later, but file that in a drawer, out of sight.

Turn Off Notifications

This is an easy step, and should only take a few minutes. You want to turn off any notifications that might interrupt you.

Email: Go to the preferences of your email program, and turn off notifications. If you have a separate program installed that notifies you of things, turn it off.

IM: Same thing with Instant Messaging/chat . . . turn off notifications. Only sign in when you're available to chat—when you want to focus, sign out, and don't have any notifications that will interrupt you.

Calendar: I'd recommend you shut off your calendar notifications as well, unless there's something you absolutely can't miss and you need the notification to remember. If something is that important, you will probably remember anyway, though.

Twitter (or other social networks): If you have a program for Twitter or any other social networks, turn it off and shut off notifications.

Mobile device: Shut off your cell phone or mobile device, if possible, when you want to truly focus. At the very least, go to the preferences of any notifications you have (email, IM, etc.) on the device and shut them off.

Phones: unplug your phone or put it on Do Not Disturb mode (or whatever it's called) when you're ready to focus.

You might have other notifications not listed here. When they pop up or make a noise, find out how to disable them. Now you can work with fewer interruptions.

Find Soothing Music and Some Headphones

Don't spend too much time on this one. If you already have music in iTunes (or whatever music program you use) or on a CD, use that. Don't spend a lot of time on the Internet researching the most relaxing music and downloading a lot of songs.

Peaceful music is great because it puts you in the right mood to focus, and it blocks out other sounds.

I'd recommend using headphones—it doesn't matter what kind—to further block out distractions. It also means coworkers are less likely to interrupt you if they see the headphones on.

Clear Your Computer Desktop

A clear desktop is not only great for your physical desk—it's great for your computer as well. Icons scattered all over a computer desktop are distracting. Instead, clear everything and be left with peace and focus.

Here's how to do it:

• *Install a launcher program.* Mac users should try either Launchbar or Quicksilver. Windows users might try Launchy or AutoHotKey (for power users). Once set up, the launcher program is activated with a keystroke combination (Command-spacebar in my case), and then you start typing the program or name of the folder or file you want to open. Usually the correct name will be automatically completed within a few keystrokes, and you press the "Return" key to activate it. It's much faster than finding the right icon on your desktop, and then double-clicking it, especially if the desktop is covered by a bunch of applications and windows.

• *Delete all application shortcuts.* Many people have shortcuts all over their desktops for commonly used applications/programs. You don't need them anymore, now that you have the launcher program. Delete them all.

• *Put all folders/files into your Documents (or My Documents) folder.* Don't worry too much about sorting them—the launcher program can find them much faster, or you could use the search function of your computer to quickly find anything you're looking for.

• *Hide everything else.* On the PC, right-click on the desktop, go to the "view" menu, and unselect "show desktop icons." On the Mac, in the Finder, go to File -> Preferences, under General, and unselect all the items under "Show these items on the Desktop." Now all your icons should be gone from the desktop.

Isn't it beautiful?

Clear Your Floor

If you have a cluttered floor surrounding your workspace, this could take awhile, so do it in chunks. No need to do everything at once.

Some people have stacks of files and papers around them. If this is you, slowly start to go through them, one file/paper at a time: do you need it? If so, file it. If not, recycle it or forward to the right person.

What else is on your floor? Quickly make decisions: do you absolutely need it? If not, get rid of it. If you do, find a place in a drawer, out of sight and not on the floor. This might mean making room in drawers by getting rid of stuff.

Again, this could take a little longer, so do it in chunks.

Clear Your Walls

Many people have calendars, pictures, memos, motivational posters, reminders, schedules, and more, hanging on their walls near their desk. Those are visual distractions and make it a little more difficult to focus. Clearing your walls, except perhaps for a nice photo or piece of art, is a good idea for creating the perfect environment for focusing.

If you've done the steps above, this one should be easy. Take everything down except for a couple of essential pieces or pleasing photos/artwork. Either get rid of things you don't need, or find an out-of-sight spot for things you do need.

14

Slowing Down

"There is more to life than increasing its speed."

–Gandhi

The world most of us live in is hectic, fast-paced, fractured, hurried.

What's more, most of us are conditioned to think this is the way life should be.

Life should be lived at break-neck speed, we believe. We risk our lives in cars and we break the speed limit, rushing from one place to another. We do one thing after another, multi-tasking and switching between tasks as fast as we can blink.

All in the name of productivity, of having more, of appearing busy, to ourselves and to others.

But life doesn't have to be this way. In fact, I'd argue that it's counterproductive.

If our goal is to create, to produce amazing things, to go for quality over quantity, then rushing is not the most effective way to work. Slowing down and focusing is always more effective.

Rushing produces errors. It's distracting to fit from one thing to the next, with our attention never on one thing long enough to give it any thought or create anything of worth. Hurrying produces too much noise to be able to find the quiet the mind needs for true creativity and profound thinking.

So yes, moving quickly will get more done. But it won't get the right things done.

Benefits of Slowing Down

There are lots of reasons to slow down, but I'll list just a few to give you an idea of why it's important:

• *Better focus.* When you slow down, you can focus better. It's hard to focus if you're moving too fast.

• *Deeper focus.* Rushing produces shallowness, because you never have time to dig beneath the surface. Slow down and dive into deeper waters.

• *Better appreciation.* You can really appreciate what you have, what you're doing, who you're with, when you take the time to slow down and really pay attention.

• *Enjoyment.* When you appreciate things, you enjoy them more. Slowing down allows you to enjoy life to the fullest.

• *Less stress.* Rushing produces anxiety and higher stress levels. Slowing down is calmer, relaxing, peaceful.

A Change of Mindset

The most important step is a realization that life is better when you move at a slower, more relaxed pace, instead of hurrying and rushing and trying to cram too much into every day. Instead, get the most out of every moment.

Is a book better if you speed read it, or if you take your time and get lost in it?

Is a song better if you skim through it, or if you take the time to really listen?

Is food better if you cram it down your throat, or if you savor every bite and really appreciate the favor?

Is your work better if you're trying to do 10 things at once, or if you really pour yourself into one important task?

Is your time spent with a friend or loved one better if you have a rushed meeting interrupted by your emails and text messages, or if you can relax and really focus on the person?

Life as a whole is better if you go slowly, and take the time to savor it, appreciate every moment. That's the simplest reason to slow down.

And so, you'll need to change your mindset (if you've been stuck in a rushed mindset until now). To do this, make the simple admission that life is better when savored, that work is better with focus. Then make the commitment to give that a try, to take some of the steps below.

But I Can't Change!

There will be some among you who will admit that it would be nice to slow down, but you just can't do it . . . your job won't allow it, or you'll lose income if you don't do as many projects, or living in the city makes it too difficult to go slowly. It's a nice ideal if you're living on a tropical island, or out in the country, or if you have a job that allows control of your schedule . . . but it's not realistic for your life.

I say bullshit.

Take responsibility for your life. If your job forces you to rush, take control of it. Make changes in what you do, in how you work. Work with your boss to make changes if necessary. And if really necessary, you can eventually change jobs. You are responsible for your life.

If you live in a city where everyone rushes, realize that you don't have to be like everyone else. You can be different. You can walk instead of driving in rush hour traffic. You can have fewer meetings. You can work on fewer but more important things. You can be on your iPhone or Blackberry less, and be disconnected sometimes. Your environment doesn't control your life—you do.

I'm not going to tell you how to take responsibility for your life, but once you make the decision, the how will become apparent over time.

Tips for a Slower-Paced Life

I can't give you a step-by-step guide to moving slower, but here are some things to consider and perhaps adopt, if they work for your life. Some things might require you to make major changes, but they can be done over time.

• *Do less.* Cut back on your projects, on your task list, on how much you try to do each day. Focus not on quantity but quality. Pick 2–3 important things—or even just one important thing—and work on those first. Save smaller, routine tasks for later in the day, but give yourself time to focus.

• *Have fewer meetings.* Meetings are usually a big waste of time. And they eat into your day, forcing you to squeeze the things you really need to do into small windows, and making you rush. Try to have blocks of time with no interruptions, so you don't have to rush from one meeting to another.

• *Practice disconnecting.* Have times when you turn off your devices and your email notifications and whatnot. Time with no phone calls, when you're just creating, or when you're just spending time with someone, or just reading a book, or just taking a walk, or just eating mindfully. You can even disconnect for (gasp!) an entire day, and you won't be hurt. I promise.

• *Give yourself time to get ready and get there.* If you're constantly rushing to appointments or other places you have to be, it's because you don't allot enough time in your schedule for preparing and for traveling. Pad your schedule to allow time for this stuff. If you think it only takes you 10 minutes to get ready for work or a date, perhaps give yourself 30–45 minutes so you don't have to shave in a rush or put on makeup in the car. If you think you can get there in 10 minutes, perhaps give yourself 2–3 times that amount so you can go at a leisurely pace and maybe even get there early.

• *Practice being comfortable with sitting, doing nothing.* One thing I've noticed is that when people have to wait, they become impatient or uncomfortable. They want their mobile device or at least a magazine, because standing and waiting is either a waste of time or something they're not used to doing without feeling self-conscious. Instead, try just sitting there, looking around, soaking in your surroundings. Try standing in line and just watching and listening to people around you. It takes practice, but after awhile, you'll do it with a smile.

• *Realize that if it doesn't get done, that's OK.* There's always tomorrow. And yes, I know that's a frustrating attitude for some of you who don't like laziness or procrastination or living without firm deadlines, but it's also reality. The world likely won't end if you don't get that task done today. Your boss might get mad, but the company won't collapse and life will inevitably go on. And the things that need to get done will.

• *Start to eliminate the unnecessary.* When you do the important things with focus, without rush, there will be things that get pushed back, that don't get done. And you need to ask yourself: how necessary are these things? What would happen if I stopped doing them? How can I eliminate them, delegate them, automate them?

• *Practice mindfulness.* Simply learn to live in the present, rather than thinking so much about the future or the past. When you eat, fully appreciate your food. When you're with someone, be with them fully. When you're walking, appreciate your surroundings, no matter where you are.

• *Slowly eliminate commitments.* We're overcommitted, which is why we're rushing around so much. I don't just mean with work—projects and meetings and the like. Parents have tons of things to do with and for their kids, and we overcommit our kids as well. Many of us have busy social lives, or civic commitments, or are coaching or playing on sports teams. We have classes and groups and hobbies. But in trying to cram so much into our lives, we're actually deteriorating the quality of those lives. Slowly eliminate commitments—pick 4–5 essential ones, and realize that the rest, while nice or important, just don't fit right now. Politely inform people, over time, that you don't have time to stick to those commitments.

Try these things out. Life is better when unrushed. And given the fleeting nature of this life, why waste even a moment by rushing through it?

15

Going with the Flow

"Life is a series of natural and spontaneous changes. Don't resist them—that only creates sorrow. Let reality be reality. Let things flow naturally forward in whatever way they like."

–Lao-Tzu

No matter how much structure we create in our lives, no matter how many good habits we build, there will always be things that we cannot control—and if we let them, these things can be a huge source of anger, frustration and stress.

The simple solution: learn to go with the flow.

For example, let's say you've created the perfect peaceful morning routine. You've structured your mornings so that you do things that bring you calm and happiness. And then a water pipe bursts in your bathroom and you spend a stressful morning trying to clean up the mess and get the pipe fixed.

You get angry. You are disappointed, because you didn't get to do your morning routine. You are stressed from all these changes to what you're used to. It ruins your day because you are frustrated for the rest of the day.

Not the best way to handle things, is it? And yet if we are honest, most of us have problems like this, with things that disrupt how we like things, with people who change what we are used to, with life when it doesn't go the way we want it to go.

Go with the flow.

What is going with the flow? It's rolling with the punches. It's accepting change without getting angry or frustrated. It's taking what life gives you, rather than trying to mold life to be exactly as you want it to be.

And what does this have to do with focusing? It's a reality that no matter how much we try to control our environment, so that we may focus on what's important, there will be interruptions and distractions. Our environment will constantly change, and we cannot completely control it.

And so, we must learn to accept this reality, and find focus within a changing environment. Here's how.

• *Realize that you can't control everything.* I think we all know this at some level, but the way we think and act and feel many times contradicts this basic truth. We don't control the universe, and yet we seem to wish we could. All the wishful thinking won't make it so. You can't even control everything within your own little sphere of influence—you can influence things, but many things are simply out of your control. In the example above, you can control your morning routine, but there will be things that happen from time to time (someone's sick, accident happens, phone call comes at 5 a.m. that disrupts things, etc.) that will make you break your routine. First step is realizing that these things will happen. Not might happen, but will. There are things that we cannot control that will affect every aspect of our lives, and we must must must accept that, or we will constantly be frustrated. Meditate on this for awhile.

• *Become aware.* You can't change things in your head if you're not aware of them. You have to become an observer of your thoughts, a self-examiner. Be aware that you're becoming upset, so that you can do something about it. It helps to keep tally marks in a little notebook for a week—every time you get upset, put a little tally. That's all—just keep tally. And soon, because of that little act, you will become more aware of your anger and frustration.

• *Breathe.* When you feel yourself getting angry or frustrated, take a deep breath. Take a few. This is an important step that allows you to calm down and do the rest of the things below. Practice this by itself and you'll have come a long way already.

• *Get perspective.* If you get angry over something happening—your car breaks down, your kids ruin something you're working on—take a deep breath, and take a step back. Let your mind's eye zoom away, until you're far away above your life. Then whatever happened doesn't seem so important. A week from now, a year from now, this little incident won't matter a single whit. No one will care, not even you. So why get upset about it? Just let it go, and soon it won't be a big deal.

• *Practice.* It's important to realize that, just like when you learn any skill, you probably won't be good at this at first. Who is good when they are first learning to write, or read, or drive? No one I know. Skills come with practice. So when you first learn to go with the flow, you will mess up. You will stumble and fall. That's OK—it's part of the process. Just keep practicing, and you'll get the hang of it.

• *Laugh.* It helps to see things as funny, rather than frustrating. Car broke down in the middle of traffic and I have no cell phone or spare tire? Laugh at my own incompetence. Laugh at the absurdity of the situation. That requires a certain amount of detachment—you can laugh at the situation if you're above it, but not within it. And that detachment is a good thing. If you can learn to laugh at things, you've come a long way. Try laughing even if you don't think it's funny—it will most likely become funny.

• *Realize that you can't control others.* This is one of the biggest challenges. We get frustrated with other people, because they don't act the way we want them to act. Maybe it's our kids, maybe it's our spouse or significant other, maybe it's our coworker or boss, maybe it's our mom or best friend. But we have to realize that they are acting according to their personality, according to what they feel is right, and they are not going to do what we want all of the time. And we have to accept that. Accept that we can't control them, accept them for who they are, accept the things they do. It's not easy, but again, it takes practice.

• *Accept change and imperfection.* When we get things the way we like them, we usually don't want them to change. But they will change. It's a fact of life. We cannot keep things the way we want them to be . . . instead, it's better to learn to accept things as they are. Accept that the world is constantly changing, and we are a part of that change. Also, instead of wanting things to be "perfect" (and what is perfect anyway?), we should accept that they will never be perfect, and we must accept good instead.

• *Enjoy life as a flow of change, chaos and beauty.* Remember when I asked what "perfect" is, in the paragraph above? It's actually a very interesting question. Does perfect mean the ideal life and world that we have in our heads? Do we have an ideal that we try to make the world conform to? Because that will likely never happen. Instead, try seeing the world as perfect the way it is. It's messy, chaotic, painful, sad, dirty . . . and completely perfect. The world is beautiful, just as it is. Life is not something static, but a flow of change, never staying the same, always getting messier and more chaotic, always beautiful. There is beauty in everything around us, if we look at it as perfect.

"A good traveler has no fixed plans, and is not intent on arriving."

–*Lao Tzu*

16

Effortless Action

"Nature does not hurry, yet everything is accomplished."

–Lao Tzu

There's a concept in Taoism, "wei wu wei," which is often translated as "action without action" or "effortless doing." I prefer to think of it more in the sense of "action that does not involve struggle or excessive effort."

This is an important concept, because effortless action is a way to not only achieve focus in a world of chaos, but to be effective without stress, to respond to any situation with economy of effort and action, and to pursue our passions while beating procrastination.

Think for a moment of times when you've struggled to work, and instead procrastinated by heading for your distractions—email, social networks, blog reading, games, whatever your favor might be.

This struggle is often a losing battle for most people. They fight against it, but only win occasionally.

Effortless action is an easier way to find focus and beat procrastination.

Be Like Water

An appropriate mental image is that of water, which seems naturally effortless in its action. It isn't necessarily still, nor is it passive, but it flows naturally around obstacles and always gets to where it's going.

This is effortless action. It uses gravity and the natural contours of its landscape, instead of forcing things. Water can never be anything but effortless, and yet it is quietly powerful.

Be like water. Flow, respond to the landscape, move around obstacles, and be graceful in your movement.

Position Yourself Effortlessly Within the Moment

In *The Civility Solution,* academic P. M. Forni writes:

"We must learn to position ourselves effortlessly within each moment, rather than stumbling through time. We can either escape from the moment or stay with it as it unfolds and do something good with it."

And this is exactly right. Are you trying to escape the moment, feeing from it and struggling against it? Or are you inhabiting the moment effortlessly?

One way to do this is to stop yourself when you find yourself struggling, and just pause. Be present, sensing your breath, and then everything around you. See the situation with some objectivity, instead of feeing from it blindly. Carefully consider your options—all of them. And then respond to the situation mindfully and with the appropriate response—not an overreaction.

In this way, you respond flexibly, appropriately, and effortlessly.

Steps for Effortless Action

There is no step-by-step guide to learning effortless action, but here are some things you might try:

• *Act because of passion.* Not because you "should," but because you're excited to do so. It will feel as if you're going downhill, because it's what you want to do.

• *When you're going uphill, change course.* Whenever you find yourself dreading something, procrastinating, forcing yourself and hating it, stop and ask yourself why. There must be a reason—you'll never sustain any action for long if you hate doing it. Change course to something you're more excited about, and things will get easier. You may end up getting to the same destination, but you'll do it with a different course and things will flow more naturally.

• *Don't try to control what you can't control.* When we try to control others, or obsessively control our surroundings, we are trying to control things that aren't in our control. This will inevitably end up in failure, frustration, and conflict with others. Instead, accept that we can't control these things, and flow around the obstacles with a minimum of effort.

• *Be in the moment.* Be aware of the full situation, accept the situation, and respond appropriately.

• *See the possibilities.* When we have our minds set, and our vision set, on one destination, we are often blind to other possibilities. We'll miss opportunities this way. Instead, see all the possible paths and pick the one that will work best for you. That doesn't mean to become indecisive because there are so many choices—to be paralyzed by choice—but instead to learn to move effortlessly among all the possible paths instead of being stuck on one path. This gets easier with practice, as you learn to trust your intuition.

• *Be flexible.* When we are rigid, we will often break. Be like water, flowing around obstacles rather than trying to push them out of your way.

• *Find the pressure points.* Sometimes, if you find the right spot, achieving something takes very little effort. Hitting a baseball with the sweet spot of the bat will cause it to go much further with less effort. Finding these spots of maximum effectiveness and minimum effort takes mindful effort, which is why effortless action isn't mindless action.

• *Do less and less, with less and less effort.* Effortless action isn't something that is achieved overnight. In fact, if you try too hard to achieve it, you've defeated yourself already. Instead, when you find yourself in a whirlwind of activity, and pushing hard, slow down, relax, and do less. Eliminate some of your motions so that you're moving with economy. Push less, and flow more. Slowly learn to do less, and then do less, finding ways of doing that require little action but lots of effectiveness. Learn to let things unfold naturally instead of pushing them to happen. Let people learn on their own instead of controlling them. Set things up so they happen without you having to steer everything. Slowly learn to use less effort, and then less than that.

• *Anticipate the difficult by managing the easy.* Another famous quote by Lao Tzu, it's timeless and wise. If you can manage the easy, small things now, you'll save yourself the time and effort of having to do the difficult things later. This allows for more effortless action—you work less to achieve the same results.

17

Three Strategies for Prioritizing Tasks

"If you chase two rabbits, both will escape."

–unknown

One of the biggest problems people have when trying to find focus is having too many tasks competing for their time. It can be tough to prioritize.

Let's break this problem into three smaller problems:

1. too many tasks
2. tough to prioritize
3. tasks compete for your time

And with that, let's discuss three strategies for dealing with these smaller problems.

1. *Reduce your tasks.* If you have too many tasks, the solution is to simplify your task list. Take 10 minutes to list everything you need to do—now just pick the 3–5 most important tasks. All the small tasks will go on a "do later" list, and you're not going to worry about them now.

A good way to deal with the smaller, routine tasks that must be done (check email, pay bills, fill out paperwork, and so on) is to schedule a block of time later in the day to deal with them—perhaps the last 30 minutes of your day, or something like that. Early in the day, focus on the important tasks.

2. *Choose the task that excites you.* Now that you've simplified your task list, look at the 3–5 tasks left and pick one task. Just one.

How do you pick? Choose the task that most excites you, that feels compelling, that you're most passionate about.

If you're dreading the task, put it aside for now, and pick something more interesting.

If you have several tasks you're excited about, you might also consider which task will have the biggest effect on your life. What will make the biggest impact?

3. *Single-task.* Now that you've chosen one task, put the others aside for now and just focus on that one task.

Clear away all distractions, including your mobile device and the Internet. Just have the application open that you need to work on that task.

Now get to work. Throw yourself into it, and do it for at least 10 minutes. After that, you can take a break, but try to immerse yourself for at least 10 minutes.

And have fun doing it.

18

Letting Go of Goals

"By letting it go it all gets done. The world is won by those who let it go. But when you try and try, the world is beyond the winning."

–Lao Tzu

One of the unshakable tenets of success and productivity literature is that you need to have goals in order to be successful. And from this tenet comes all sorts of other beliefs:

- You need to set goals the right way (such as the SMART method).
- You need to break goals down into actionable tasks.
- You need to have deadlines and timeframes.
- You need to make goals the focus of your day.

I know this, because I've believed it and lived it and written about it, for a long time.

Until recently.

Until recently, I'd always set goals for myself—short-term and long-term ones, with action lists. I've made progress on each one, and accomplished a lot of goals. And from this traditional viewpoint, I've been successful. So no argument there: goals work, and you can be successful using goals.

But are they the only way?

More recently I've moved away from goals, broken free of the shackles of goals. I've liberated myself because goals are not ideal, in my way of thinking:

• They are artificial—you aren't working because you love it, you're working because you've set goals.

• They're constraining—what if you want to work on something not in line with your goals? Shouldn't we have that freedom?

• They put pressure on us to achieve, to get certain things done. Pressure is stressful, and not always in a good way.

• When we fail (and we always do), it's discouraging.

• We're always thinking about the future (goals) instead of the present. I prefer to live in the present.

But most of all, here's the thing with goals: you're never satisfied. Goals are a way of saying, "When I've accomplished this goal (or all these goals), I will be happy then. I'm not happy now, because I haven't achieved my goals." This is never said out loud, but it's what goals really mean. The problem is, when we achieve the goals, we don't achieve happiness. We set new goals, strive for something new.

And while many people will say that striving for something new is a good thing, that we should always be striving, unfortunately it means we're never satisfied. We never find contentment. I think that's unfortunate—we should learn how to be content now, with what we have. It's what minimalism is all about, really.

And if my philosophy is to be happy now, with enough, with the present, then how are goals consistent with this? It's something I've tried to reconcile over the last few years, with some success.

So if we are content now, and we abandon goals, does that mean we do nothing? Sit around or sleep all day?

Not at all. I certainly don't do that. We should do what makes us happy, follow our passions, do things that make us excited. For me and many people, that's creating, building new things, expressing ourselves, making something useful or new or beautiful or inspiring.

So here's what I do, instead of setting and achieving goals:

• I do what excites me. Each day. I wake up, and work on things that I'm passionate about, create things that I love creating.

• I don't worry about where I'll be (professionally) in a year or even six months, but where I am right now.

• I don't make plans, because they're an illusion—you never know what will happen in a year or even six months. You can try to control what happens, but you'll lose. Things always come up, sometimes good and sometimes bad, that will disrupt plans. Instead, I've learned to go with the flow, to not worry about things that disrupt plans but worry about what to do right now. This allows me to take advantage of opportunities that come up that I could never have planned for, to work on things I couldn't have known about, to make decisions about what's best right now, not what I planned a few months ago.

• I don't force things, but do what comes naturally. And I focus on the present, on being happy now.

This has taken me time—letting go of goals is a scary and uncomfortable thing, but if you let them go gradually, it's not that hard. I've slowly adapted the way I work, and learned to work in the moment, and go with the flow of the world that surrounds me (online and off).

It's a beautiful way of working. And not incidentally, I've accomplished even more this way, without making that a goal. It's a natural byproduct of doing what you love.

"A good traveler has no fixed plans, and is not intent on arriving."

–Lao Tzu

19

Finding Simplicity

"Perfection is achieved, not when there is nothing more to add, but when there is nothing left to take away."

–Antoine de Saint-Exupéry

For years now I have been working on living a simpler life—in my personal, family and work life. It's been one of the best things I've ever done, in many ways:

• A simple life is less stressful, more sane, happier.

• Simpler living is less expensive, which helped me to get out of debt.

• I'm able to focus better when I work, leading to a more successful career than ever (by far).

• I free up time for my family, and for the things I love most. I've rid my life of things I didn't like doing.

• I have fewer possessions, leading to a less cluttered home and workspace, which I love.

And those are just a few of the benefits. When it comes to finding focus, simplifying is a great place to start. When you simplify, you remove the extraneous and allow yourself to focus. You might say that simplifying is a necessary part of finding focus.

This is a short guide to finding simplicity.

Simplifying Your Life

What does a simplified life look like? There's no one answer. While some might go to the extremes of living in a cabin in Alaska or on a tropical island, others find simplicity in a city while working a job with the hectic pace of a stockbroker. The key is to find what matters most to you, and to eliminate as much of the rest as possible.

A simpler life probably means fewer possessions. We allow ourselves to accumulate possessions through years of shopping, receiving gifts, and so on, until we're overwhelmed by it all. We are strongly influenced by advertising to acquire things, but we don't have a good system for getting rid of them. Freeing yourself of clutter leaves room for thinking, for focus.

A simpler life means fewer commitments. This is difficult, as commitments accumulate over the years just as much as possessions do, and the result is that we have no time in our lives for what really matters. Getting out of the commitments you already have is the painful part: it requires saying "no" to people, disappointing them in some way. In my experience, they'll live, and life will go on. And when you've eliminated many of your commitments, you've freed up so much of your time for things you truly love.

A simpler life means less distractions, less busy-ness, less clutter . . . and more space for what matters most to you. You free up time for work you're passionate about, people you love, hobbies that make you happy. Time for solitude, for thinking. And that's a good thing.

Simplifying Your Work

Simplifying work is very similar to simplifying your life in general, but a bit more "productivity" oriented of course. Let's start with this question: what does it mean to simplify your work?

It can mean a lot of things, including:

• Clearing the clutter of your workspace, to give you a distraction-free and more soothing space to find focus.

• Focusing less on busy-work and more on important work that has a high impact on your career and business.

• Working on fewer projects and tasks so you're less busy, and more focused.

• Narrowing the scope of your work so you do less but do it better, offer less but offer better things.

• Eliminating streams of communication, news, distractions.

• Creating the work life you want, rather than one that is a reaction to requests and needs of others.

For me, that means waking in the morning and deciding on one thing that's most important for me to work on. It means spending less time on email and other distractions, and more time on creating and important tasks. It means having a distraction-free workspace and time and room for thinking. It's a work life that I love, and recommend to anyone.

A simplified work life can be difficult for a couple of reasons, though:

• *You have to learn to say "no" to others.* By saying "yes" to every request from others, you allow all your time to be taken up by tasks that are important to others, not necessarily to you. Saying "no" means being tough, and valuing your time above all else. It can be uncomfortable to say "no" sometimes, but the result is more room for what's important, and less busy-ness.

• *You should also try to learn to do less.* This is difficult for most people, because we're taught that doing more means we're more productive, and if we look busy, people will think we're productive and important. And yet, it's not true. Being busy doesn't mean a thing, other than we're stressed out. We could be busy doing meaningless tasks. Doing important work is what true productivity is all about, and that doesn't necessarily mean we're ridiculously busy. Focus on fewer but higher-impact tasks.

How to Get Started

With all of this clutter in our lives to simplify, it can be overwhelming, daunting, to even get started. Don't let that stop you—getting started is more important than doing everything at once, or starting in exactly the right place.

There are two things I'd recommend you do to get started—and you can choose which one to do first, as it doesn't matter really where you start:

• *Pick your life's short list.* It's crucial that you take a step back and figure out what's most important to you. I suggest taking half a day off, or even just 30–60 minutes. Get outside and take a walk, or go to a coffee shop, and allow yourself to think. Big picture stuff: what do you love most? Every person's list will be different—my list was: spending time with family, writing, reading and running. Pick just 4–5 things, even if there are lots of other things that also seem important. Now make a longer list: what else is in your life that's not on the short list? Once you've done these things, you're done with the Big Picture stuff—the next step is to start eliminating commitments that aren't on the short list. Do the same for your work life—what's most important, and what doesn't make your short list of most important projects and goals?

• *Start clearing clutter in one spot.* Physical clutter can be overwhelming, which is why you should just pick one small spot, and clear that. You can get to the rest later. It might be the top of your desk, or if that is super messy maybe just one spot on top of your desk. It might be a table-top or part of a counter or shelf in your home. It doesn't matter what the spot is. Here's how to start: first clear off that area and put everything into a pile to the side. Now sort through the pile quickly, making three smaller piles: stuff you use and love, stuff you can donate, and trash. Sort quickly and ruthlessly—everything should go in one of the three piles. Then throw the trash away, put the donate stuff in a box to be dropped off to a charity, and put the stuff you love and use neatly where it belongs. Everything should have a permanent home. Done! Slowly expand your decluttered zone.

How to Systematically Simplify

Once you've gotten started with the two things above, take this newly found momentum and keep it going. You don't need to do it all at once—20 minutes a day would do wonders. Small steps, one at a time.

Here's what I'd do, in little chunks:

• *Take 10 minutes a day to clear another small area of clutter.* It could be another area on top of your desk or a table, it could be a drawer, a shelf, a counter, a small area of the floor, a wall that's covered in papers in your office. Follow the sorting method above. Expand the decluttered zone daily.

• *Take 10 minutes a day to simplify your commitments, what you do, and what comes into your life.* Just simplify one or two things a day. If you choose a commitment to eliminate, simply call or email someone, letting them know you can no longer serve on this committee or that board, or coach this team or play on that one, or work on this project or that. If you choose to simplify what you do, cross things off your to-do list that aren't on your short list—sometimes that means emailing someone to let them know you can't work on it because your plate is too full. If you choose what comes into your life, you might eliminate an email newsletter that you get daily (or all newsletters), you might pare down your blog reading list, or unsubscribe from a magazine, or stop using a social service or forum that doesn't add value to your life.

In this way, one little chunk at a time, you'll eventually clear a lot of the physical and mental clutter in your personal and work life, and things will get simpler over time.

Section IV

Focus

20

A Simple System for Getting Amazing Things Done

"Do whatever you do intensely."

–Robert Henri

If all of the chapters and tips in this book overwhelm you, don't worry. You can read this chapter alone and it'll be sufficient. This chapter outlines my current way of working, and it's a simple system for Getting Amazing Things Done.

In fact, it's three simple steps. It can't get any easier.

Step 1: Find Something Amazing to Work On

Every day, first thing in the morning, figure out Something Amazing that you want to work on today.

It can be anything: a big project at work, creating your own business, learning programming or web development skills, writing a song, taking photographs, anything. It should be something that excites you, that will change your life at least in some small way. It should compel you to work on it because you're inspired, excited, motivated.

Some people are lucky enough to know what that is every day. I'm one of those: I love writing, and I always have some blog post or book to write (often too many to choose from). I just need to choose the particular thing to write about.

Others haven't found their passion yet, and that's OK. You don't need to make a huge life decision today. All you need to do is pick something that sounds fun—it could be a project you have at work, or a potential hobby, or

learning a new skill, or learning how to start your own business. It doesn't matter what you pick—because if you're wrong, you can pick something different tomorrow.

Some ideas—but not by any means an exhaustive list—of what Something Amazing might be:

• A manifesto that will change your business, industry, or personal life.

• An exciting new way of reaching potential customers.

• That great novel you always wanted to write.

• A screenplay, play, short story, new type of fiction. A blog post that will help others.

• A new non-profit organization to help others.

• A lesson that will wow your students.

• A craft activity that your kids will get a thrill out of.

• A community garden to share with your neighbors.

• A new invention, an idea for a website, an improvement on a classic idea.

• Crazy new fashion, beautiful clothes, hand-crafted jewelry.

• Philosophy.

• Poetry.

• Wooden furniture.

• Ikebana.

• Something beautiful. Something profound. Something life-changing.

• Something small, but that will have some kind of impact.

• Something that improves the lives of others.

• Something that changes your own life.

• Something that simplifies to the essential.

You get the idea. It can be almost anything.

You're not locking yourself in to this choice for life—just for today, or at least a little bit of today. Try something out, see how it goes. You never know if you're going to find the thing that changes your life.

Step 2: Clear Away Everything Else

Here's the thing that will help you achieve that something amazing: clearing away distractions.

You're going to clear your desk—shove everything in a drawer or box if you have to, and leave only the papers necessary to work on your Something Amazing, and a couple of other essential items (phone, pen & pad, etc.).

You're going to clear your computer—close all programs, including your browser, that you don't absolutely need for this task. It's also crucial that you turn off all notifications on your computer that might distract you: email notifications, Instant Messaging (IM), calendar notifications, anything. Make your computer as distraction-free as possible.

Also turn off your phone, Blackberry, iPhone, and anything else that might distract you from your Something Amazing.

Finally, clear away meetings and anything on your task list that will interfere with this one task. You can get to those other tasks later, but for now, you're going to work on nothing but this one amazing task.

Step 3: Focus on That Something Amazing

OK, everything is clear. Now you just need to focus on that Something Amazing—that one task you chose that you're excited about, that's going to change your life in some small way.

Do this as soon as you can in the day—not after lunch or late in the day, but as close to First Thing as you can. Either before you go into work or as soon as you get into work and can clear your desk. Don't wait until later, or things will pile up and you'll never get to it.

This is actually the step that most people have a problem with. They get the urge to check email or make that phone call or . . .

do anything else, really. No! Stop yourself, take a deep breath, and remember why you chose this task. You're excited about it. Feel that excitement, and focus.

Even if that focus only comes for a few minutes, give it your best shot. You might give in to the urge to do something else, but then bring yourself back and see if you can't focus for a few more minutes. Repeat until you've worked a good chunk (30 minutes, an hour, two hours, half the day if possible) on your Something Amazing.

Do your best to either finish this Something Amazing, or a good chunk of it. If it's a big project that will take days, months or years, just finish a chunk that'll take at least an hour or two of your day.

When you're done, bask in the glory of your accomplishment.

If you have more time and energy, repeat the process. Work on your next Something Amazing. Keep doing this, working on exciting and amazing things, for the rest of your life.

21

Single-Tasking and Productivity

"Concentrate all your thoughts upon the work at hand. The sun's rays do not burn until brought to a focus."

–Alexander Graham Bell

Many of us grew up in the age of multi-tasking, where you couldn't call yourself productive if you weren't a good multi-tasker. We learned to always have several balls in the air at once—while writing something on the computer, we had a phone call going, we were writing something on a notepad or paper form, we were reviewing documents, sometimes even holding a meeting at the same time. That's the productive worker, the effective executive.

When email and Instant Messaging and blogs and the rest of the Internet came along, multi-tasking went haywire. Now we're expected to do 10 things on the computer at once, still with the paper, phone, and meetings going, along with texting and Blackberry Messaging. Multi-tasking is no longer about being productive—it's a way of living.

It's not a sane way of living, however, and it's not necessarily the most effective way of working either. A few notes on why:

• Multi-tasking is less efficient, due to the need to switch gears for each new task, and then switch back again.

• Multi-tasking is more complicated, and thus more prone to stress and errors.

• Multi-tasking can be crazy, and in this already chaotic world, we need to reign in the terror and find a little oasis of sanity and calm.

Our brains can really only handle one thing at a time, and so we get so used to switching between one thing and another with our brains that we program them to have a short attention span. This is why it's so hard to learn to focus on one thing at a time again.

A Single-Tasking Life

Imagine instead, a single-tasking life. Imagine waking and going for a run, as if running were all you do. Nothing else is on your mind but the run, and you do it to the very best of your abilities. Then you eat, enjoying every flavorful bite of your fresh breakfast of whole, unprocessed foods. You read a novel, as if nothing else in the world existed. You do your work, one task at a time, each task done with full focus and dedication. You spend time with loved ones, as if nothing else existed.

This is summed up very well by something Charles Dickens once wrote: "He did each single thing as if he did nothing else." This is a life lived fully in the moment, with a dedication to doing the best you can in anything you do—whether that's a work project or making green tea.

If you live your life this way, by this single principle, it will have tremendous effects:

• Your work will become more focused.

• You will become more effective at your work. » You'll become better at anything you do. » Your time alone will be of better quality.

• Your time with your family will be much more meaningful.

• Your reading will have less distractions.

• You'll lose yourself in anything you deem worthy enough of your time and attention.

How to Live a Single-Tasking Life

It sounds nice, but how do you live a life like this? Is it as simple as saying you're going to do it, or is it impossible? Somewhere in between, of course, and like anything worth doing, it takes practice.

Here's what I'd recommend:

• *Become conscious.* When you start doing something, become more aware you're starting that activity. As you do it, become aware of really doing it, and of the urge to switch to something else. Paying attention is the important first step.

• *Clear distractions.* If you're going to read, clear everything else away, so you have nothing but you and the book. If you're going to do email, close every other program and all browser tabs except the email tab, and just do that. If you're going to do a work task, have nothing else open, and turn off the phone. If you're going to eat, put away the computer and other devices and shut off the television.

• *Choose wisely.* Don't just start doing something. Give it some thought—do you really want to turn on the TV? Do you really want to do email right now? Is this the most important work task you can be doing?

• *Really pour yourself into it.* If you're going to make tea, do it with complete focus, complete dedication. Put everything you have into that activity. If you're going to have a conversation, really listen, really be present. If you're going to make your bed, do it with complete attention and to the best of your abilities.

• *Practice.* This isn't something you'll learn to do overnight. You can start right now, but you're not likely to be good at it at first. Keep at it. Practice daily, throughout the day. Do nothing else, but practice.

Single-Tasking Productivity

While the above tips will apply to work tasks as well as life in general, here are some tips focused more on productivity at work:

• *Pick just a few tasks each day.* While you might keep a longer master list of things to do, each day you should make a short list—just

1–3 things you really want to accomplish. Call this your Most Important Task (MIT) list. These should be extremely important tasks that will have a high-impact on your life.

• *Don't do anything else before doing the first thing on your short list of MITs.* Don't check email, Facebook, Twitter, blogs, online forums, news sites. Start your day after making your short list by working on your first MIT.

• *Clear distractions.* Shut off phones, close the browser if possible, close your IM program if you have one, even disconnect your Internet if you can stand it.

• *Do one task at a time.* Keep things simple, focused and effective by single-tasking. Focus on one task until it's done, then move to the next.

• *If you feel the urge to check your email or switch to another task, stop yourself.* Breathe deeply. Re-focus yourself. Get back to the task at hand.

• *Keep on your MITs until you're done.* Then you have time for email, paperwork, routine tasks, etc. Or if you have the time, pick another set of MITs.

• *If other things come up, note them on a piece of paper or small notebook.* These are notes for things to do or follow-up on later, or ideas. Just take a short note, and then get back to your MIT. This way you don't get sidetracked, but you also don't forget those things you need to remember later.

• *Take deep breaths, stretch, and take breaks now and then.* Enjoy life. Go outside, and appreciate nature. Keep yourself sane.

Keep a very short to-do list, clear distractions, do one thing at a time, until the list is finished. That's single-tasking productivity at its essence.

On Multi-Projecting

There's a distinction between tasks and projects that should be made in any discussion of multi-tasking. Doing multiple tasks at the same time is less effective than single-tasking. But doing multiple projects at once is sometimes more effective than only one project at once.

Sometimes it's necessary to work on multiple projects—even if you are in complete control of your work, which is not true for many people. If you only work on one project at once, often you are held up because you're waiting for somebody to do a task or reply to you with necessary information. What happens then? Or what happens if you're collaborating on a project but while someone else is doing their part, you don't have much to do? In these cases, it would probably be a waste of your time if you just waited, and worked on nothing else.

So multi-projecting can work—you get one project going, but while you're waiting on something, you can switch to a second or even third project. All the time, you're only working on one task at a time, until each task is done, however.

Do note that there's a danger in taking on too many projects at once. I'd suggest taking on as few projects as possible. If you can do only one project at a time, without getting stuck in waiting, then do that—it's much more effective and you'll get your projects done much faster. But when you must wait, you can switch to a second project. Again, work on as few at a time as you can get away with.

22

The Power of a Smaller Work Focus

"Success demands singleness of purpose."

–Vince Lombardi

When you set your sights on a large target, broad in scope, you spread yourself thin. This is why the best companies are those with a laser focus. They do less, but they do it better.

Apple is a good example of this—they don't try to tackle every computer niche. They don't make netbooks or low-end PCs, for example. They have a very small product line for such a big company. And yet, they do extremely well—they make beautiful, well-made, high-functioning devices that customers absolutely love. And they make billions to boot. That's just one example of many.

A narrower focus allows you to do a better job—to be better than anyone else, perhaps, at the narrower thing that you're good at.

The Danger of a Broad Focus

One of the biggest problems many people have in their careers, with work projects, with their businesses, is too broad of a focus. Just a few examples:

• Working on too many projects and trying to juggle your time between all of them.

- Adding too many features to your software and creating a bloated application.
- Trying to do everything for every customer, and spreading yourself too thin.
- Trying to be everything for everybody, but ending up being nothing good.
- Trying to please all your bosses and coworkers and forgetting what's important.
- Communicating all the time via email, several social networks, phones, text messaging, cell phones, faxes and more . . . and never communicating with any depth.

Again, there are lots of other ways to have a focus that's too broad. In the end, it's a choice between trying to do everything but doing it poorly, or doing only a tiny amount of things really well.

Take Stock

What's your current focus at work? Are you a writer involved in a whole range of writing projects at once? Are you a developer trying to offer something that appeals to everyone and solves every problem? Do you try to satisfy every possible customer, even if most of those possibilities are the exception rather than the rule?

Whatever your focus, take a closer look at it. What do you focus on that's absolutely essential, and what isn't as important? Figure out your top priorities, and also think about how much time you allocate to each of these focuses.

What are the possibilities of narrowing your focus? Of dropping some features or catering to a smaller group of customers or doing fewer things for fewer people? How hard would that be? What would need to be done to make that happen?

Narrowing Focus

Now that you've identified your top priorities, the hard part is done. Not that narrowing focus is always easy—especially when you have team members or management involved who don't quite get it.

In that case, it'll take some convincing. Show them examples of companies or projects that excelled with a smaller focus, and the problems of too broad a focus.

Be unrelenting.

If you have control over your focus, and the focus of what you work on, you're lucky. Now it just takes some guts, and perhaps some time. You don't need to change everything overnight. That's the power of small changes—you can slowly narrow your focus. Slowly do less, one thing at a time, and you'll see how it can transform your work.

When you drop one feature at a time, do one less type of service, do one fewer project at a time . . . it's not so hard. And the improvements that come with the smaller focus will encourage you to continue to simplify, until you've found the smallest focus that works for you.

23

Focused Reading and Research

"A book is like a garden carried in the pocket."

—Chinese Proverb

Focused reading is something that's becoming a rarer and rarer animal these days. We have a hard time reading even a single blog post if it's not a simple list or longer than a couple hundred words—we'll skim, and then move on to the next post or email.

Our reading habits have changed because of the persistence and ubiquity of online distractions. We read shorter, faster, more frequently, but longer reading is dwindling. Focused reading is harder.

One effect is that we're reading fewer books and longer articles, and more blogs and shorter articles. Another effect is that any research we need to do is filled with distractions—landmines when it comes to getting work done.

However, it's not impossible to read or do research with focus. Just harder.

How to Read Longer Pieces Without Distractions

There are two keys to reading longer pieces or books: 1) clearing away everything else, and 2) shutting off the Internet.

Without those two things, you'll always have distractions. Even if you do manage to do those two things, the siren's call of messages and other updates are still tempting.

For reading longer articles or blog posts, I'll put the article/post in a separate window, without other tabs to distract me. I'll expand that window to cover my entire screen. And then I'll turn off the Internet, so nothing else calls while I read.

Then I just read, until I get to the end (or until I realize this article isn't worth my time). I don't switch to another window or program until I'm done.

There's something peaceful about this process. It's saying: I have nothing else to do but read this one thing. Nothing is going to interrupt me, and I can just focus on enjoying this reading.

Book reading is the same way. If you're reading a physical book, you need to put away your laptop and mobile devices, and shut everything off. Find a quiet place, and just read. If you're reading an ebook, clear away everything else but your ebook reader.

Then you settle into the reading, and enjoy it. Bask in the luxury of reading without distractions.

How to Do the Research Necessary for Focused Creation

Research can be more of a challenge, because you need to be connected to find information, usually. You'll want to do Google searches and then follow links within the first batch of articles you find, and so on. The nature of research tends to require link-following.

Here's the method I suggest for more focused research:

1. Close email/IM/social networks and other distractions.

2. Do your initial search, and open up your initial batch of articles/ pages.

3. Skim these articles/pages, looking for links to other articles you might need to read. Open those links.

4. Repeat with the new articles, skimming and opening links as necessary. Do this until you have all the articles open you need to read.

5. Read one article at a time, using the method in the previous section—opening that article in its own window and hiding everything else. Read through the article, and take any notes necessary. Bookmark the article if necessary for later reference.

6. Repeat, taking notes and bookmarking one article at a time. When your research is done, you can do the actual work, using the focus techniques for work in the other chapters of this book.

24

Walking, Disconnection, and Focus

"An early-morning walk is a blessing for the whole day."

–Henry David Thoreau

The simple act of walking can be a tremendous boost to your focus, productivity, clarity of mind, not to mention your health and waistline. Recently a fellow blogger wrote to me talking about how many pounds she lost on vacation because she walked all day long—something many of us have experienced. She ended by saying, "If only I could find the time to walk 6 hours a day."

That got me to ask—why not? Why can't we work out a routine where we walk all day long?

What follows are a couple of radical but incredibly fulfilling and productive changes from most people's daily routine. I think they're worthy of consideration if you:

- have any control over your schedule;
- can work from different locations;
- want to get more active and trim your waistline; and
- need to find new ways to focus and get important things done.

I recently tried both these routines and loved them, and am working them into my life in different ways.

1. The Walking Vacation Working Routine

I love going on vacation, not only for the food and sights and history and culture and people, but for the walking. You get in amazing shape by walking around all day, exploring, taking frequent breaks but staying on your feet for at least half the day.

Why should we reserve this fantastic routine to vacations? Just because we need to get work done?

Consider a routine that consists of alternating short walks with work:

1. Walk for 20–30 minutes to a location: coffee shop, library, park, beach, cafe or bistro, peaceful rest spot, etc. Don't use mobile devices as you walk—remain disconnected.

2. Work or read for 30–40 minutes: write, take notes, read, respond to emails, design, meet with a colleague or client, make calls, whatever. You can also have coffee, some water, fruits, a small meal, and so on.

3. Repeat as many times as you can.

This is a bit of a nomadic work schedule, roaming from one place to another, but it has numerous benefits:

• When you walk, you can think, which is something that's hard to do when you're sitting and distracted all day. When you get to your destination, write down all the notes from your walking contemplation.

• When you walk, you can also clear your head, meditate, or just enjoy your surroundings and relieve stress.

• You get into tremendous shape by walking so much.

• Your work will also be more focused, because you have less time to work. Use the 30–40 minute bursts of work for important tasks that you think about as you walk.

• Some stops can be in spots without a wireless connection, which means you'll get more work done without the distraction of the Internet.

2. The Disconnect and Connect Working Routine

A number of people have announced vacations from the Internet, when they go a few days or a week or even a month without any connection—on purpose. This serves as a way for them to reconnect with life, to find focus and get important things done, and to enjoy the peace of disconnection.

But why make it an occasional "cleanse"? Why not build it into your routine?

Consider a routine such as the following:

Disconnect for a day (or two). No Internet connection—perhaps no computer at all if using your computer is too much of a temptation to connect. Use an actual paper notepad and pen, writing and brainstorming and making pages of notes or sketches. Make phone calls instead of connecting via email or IM. Meet with people in real life, and get outside. Get a ton of important work done. No mobile devices except for actual phone calls.

Then connect for a day (or two). Take all the notes and work you did during your disconnect, and type them up and email them and post them online and so forth. Answer emails and get other routine tasks done, and then prepare for your next day of disconnect.

Repeat. You can vary the number of days you're disconnected or connected, finding the balance that works for you.

While some may feel this will limit the work they can do, I think it'll actually do the opposite: you'll get more done, or at least more important tasks done, because you won't be distracted.

You'll also find it a calming change from the always-connected. It's a peaceful routine.

Conclusions

The purpose of these two routines isn't to tell you how to work, because we must each find the style and routine that works for our particular job. It's to show you that change is possible, and that if you think outside the usual, you can find some exciting possibilities.

You don't need to do these things exactly the way I've outlined above, but you can find a blend that works best for you. Perhaps a hybrid routine that uses both concepts, or a once-a-week walking or disconnect period.

Integrating walking into your work routine can do wonders for your fitness and for your focus. That's something you can't find if you're sitting all day.

Integrating disconnection into your work routine will allow you to get even more done, and to find peace of mind.

I urge you to consider both, and see how they can make your life better.

Section V

Others

25

Finding Focus, for Parents

"The field of consciousness is tiny. It accepts only one problem at a time."

–Antoine de Saint-Exupéry

Parents might have the most difficult challenges when it comes to finding focus. Whether you're working all day and coming home to your kids, or you stay home taking care of all the household needs and very demanding children, there's almost never a quiet moment, almost never a time when you can relax, find focus, attain inner peace.

I'm a father of six children, so I know. Kids tend to turn up the volume on life, increase the chaos of this already chaotic world by an order of several magnitudes. And while I've found that it gets easier as kids get older, it never gets easy—they still need you to drive them around a million places, to help them with a million problems, to meet their basic needs and more.

That's OK—chaos and work are some of the joys of being a parent. But what if we want to find focus and still be awesome parents? There's the challenge, and I'd like to offer a short guide to doing just that.

The Challenges

The biggest challenge is that parents wear many hats: we have jobs, have a household to run with its unending tasks, have personal things to do (workout, read, hobbies, etc.), possibly have civic commitments (volunteer, serve on a board, work with the PTA, etc.), and yes, we have children to raise.

How do we balance these commitments? How do we find focus in one, when we are constantly being pulled at from the others? In my life, for example, I try to focus on work but have children in my home/office who want my attention. When I spend time with them, there's the temptation to check email or Twitter. When I want to spend time alone, the siren's call of work and the never-ending call of my children make focusing on my solo activity a challenge.

Technology presents yet another challenge. Parents these days are connected more than ever. Not only are we online more than ever before, we now have devices that keep us connected wherever we go: iPhones and Androids and Blackberries and iPads and laptops and iPod touches. While our teenager is texting us, we're getting work emails, along with requests from our civic commitments, and a notification of a blog post about our favorite hobby.

Children make a parent's attempt to find focus a bigger challenge than usual. People without children aren't likely to understand this, so we're not given breaks by our bosses or colleagues—saying that you had to take your kid to the dentist, or that your baby kept you up all night crying, isn't likely to get you off the hook. After all, we signed up to be parents, didn't we?

Still, it's uniquely difficult: there isn't a minute, it seems, when our kids don't need something, or have a problem, or want attention, or have an appointment or practice they need to be taken to. And if there are moments when they're not requiring our attention, often we're thinking about things we need to be doing with them, for them. We're thinking about what we should be doing but aren't: reading to them more, taking them to parks to play, teaching them to build or garden or write, working on craft projects, taking them to museums, handing down the key lessons in life.

It ain't easy. But you knew that.

One Approach

With so many hats, an effective way to find focus is to segregate your roles. Block them off into separate chunks of your day or week. And then focus on each individually, whenever possible.

So set aside certain times of your day for different roles, and block out distractions from the other roles.

An example:

• Early mornings: wake early, before the kids are up, and spend time with yourself. Go for a run, meditate, do yoga, read a novel. Or use this time for creating: draw, design, write, etc.

• Mid mornings: When the kids are up, help them get ready for school, get yourself ready for work, get lunches packed, etc. This is your time as a parent, and don't do anything work-related. Talk with your kids if you find a moment.

• Later mornings: Set aside for work. If you work from home, don't do any household duties.

• Afternoon: Do the household duties. Or more work. Late afternoon: Spend time with kids. Block out work.

• Early evening: Some personal time. Let the kids do their homework, and you focus on yourself.

• Late evening: Read to your child, spend a little quiet time with her, put her to bed.

Obviously this is just an example, and won't work for everyone. You'll need to find the schedule that works for you. Perhaps you work best in the evenings, or you can't do any work until your spouse gets home to take care of the kids, or you need to spend time with the kids all morning. There's no One Size Fits All when it comes to parenting, but to the extent that you can block off your day, it helps.

You'll also need to be flexible. It can be a problem when someone is so fixed on a daily routine that disruptions to the routine—a last minute meeting, a call from your kids' school that your daughter is sick—will cause anxiety. As parents, of course, we learn to adapt, to deal with interruptions and changes. We need to calmly accept changes to our schedule, but as we switch to a new role (parenting, work, personal, civic, etc.), we need to learn to do only that role, again to the extent possible.

Very Young Children

I should note that it's harder for parents of babies and toddlers. The younger the child, in general, the more demanding on your attention the child can be. That's not a hard-and-fast rule, of course, but in my experience (I have six kids), it gets easier to focus on other things as the child gets older.

So how do you segregate roles and find focus when your child is young and always demands your attention? It's not easy, I'll say that. The best solution involves both parents pitching in, and giving the other a break once or twice a day. So instead of both parents taking care of the child, they take turns, and one gets some quiet time for a walk, reading, work, creating, hobbies, exercise. Then they switch.

Of course, there are also naptimes. If your baby is so young that you're not getting very much sleep, you'll probably want to rest when your baby rests. But otherwise, take advantage of naptimes and get some "you" stuff done. Take advantage of the quiet times, too, in the early morning before your child is awake, and at night when the child has gone to sleep.

Another solution is to get help: a professional babysitter, daycare for half a day, one of your parents who might be retired, a niece or nephew who is trustworthy and has a couple hours after school. While some of these solutions will cost some money, it might be worth the expense. You might also find another parent who needs help, and swap babysitting.

On Technology

Parents who are used to being connected in some ways might be better off by learning to embrace disconnection.

Imagine you're taking a walk in the park with your child . . . it's a lovely day, and it's the perfect quiet moment between you and your young one. Then your phone beeps, and you know you have a new email. Well, you've been waiting for something from the boss or client, so you have the urge to check. It's just going to take a few seconds—no problem right?

Well, it's a problem. This small distraction takes you from the moment with your child, and back to the world of work. It ruins it, even if only slightly. It also teaches your child that this email is more important than she is—you can't make the effort to be totally present with your child, because of important work emails. That's not the best message to send.

I don't mean to be preachy—I'm guilty of these distractions from time to time too. But it's something we should become aware of and if possible, take measures against. Turn off the phone, shut off notifications, and be present.

When you're at home, you can be on the computer all the time, while your child is calling for attention. Turn the computer off for stretches of time, and give your undivided attention to your child. When it's time to work, or create, find a way to do so without the interruptions of children, and focus. But the rest of the time, shut off the computer.

26

The Problem of Others

In a perfect world, you could learn to beat the urges that defeat you and create an environment of focus . . . and just focus. But we live and work in a world with other people, and that can make finding focus difficult.

Often, our lives aren't completely under our control. Sometimes, others can stand in our way, or just make things tough. Often other people can make a big impact on our ability to simplify and create. Let's take a look at some of those types of situations, and some solutions that can help.

Service Industries

If you work in a service industry, finding focus by cutting out all distractions might seem impossible. After all, you have to respond to customers pretty much immediately, and ignoring them in person or not responding to their calls or emails isn't really an option. Someone in the service industry must be on their toes, and work non-stop, often multitasking the whole time.

Sure, but there are some choices:

• *While you're serving customers, do only that.* Don't also deal with other problems, if possible, or work on other tasks. Be in the moment as much as possible, dealing with each customer while fully present. You'll do a better job for the customer and connect much more deeply on a human level. It's hard to do well on a customer call if you're also dealing with emails, or serve a customer in person well if you're also looking at your iPhone.

• *Try to serve one customer at a time.* This isn't always possible either, but when you can do it, it's much better—for the customer and for your sanity levels. Deal with one customer's email at a time, one call at a time, one customer in person at a time. When possible.

• *Find some time on the job for focus.* If you have other things to do than deal directly with customers, try to separate the two responsibilities, so that you can deal with customers during one part of your day and find focus during another part of your day. Even if it's just for 30–60 minutes, clearing distractions can make a big difference.

• *Find ways to reduce the load.* While customer problems and requests are always important, there are ways to reduce the demands on your time. Automating is a good example—allow people to order or file something online, for example, instead of fling the orders with you manually, or find other online solutions to the things you handle on a regular basis. Putting up a Frequently Asked Questions on a website can help reduce problems and questions. Outsourcing customer calls might be an option. Narrowing your services can help. All of these are dependent on you having control over the business, but if you do, consider the many alternatives that might reduce your workload and interruptions.

• *Find focus in your personal life.* If most of your life is spent dealing with non-stop customer problems, complaints and requests, then you might try to find a time for calm, without distractions. Don't be connected all the time, don't be on the phone or doing text messages—cut off from the distractions, slow down, find solitude, and let your mind rest.

Staff/Co-Workers Interruptions

If you have staff or co-workers who rely on you, you might be constantly interrupted (in person, by phone, via instant messages, by email) by people who need decisions made, conflicts managed, problems solved, requests fulfilled.

So how do we find focus with these kinds of constant, urgent interruptions? There are many possible solutions, and not all will apply to everyone, but here are some ideas:

• *Remove yourself as a bottleneck.* It's almost impossible to find a moment of peace when all decisions, all problems, must come through you. So train others to make these decisions. Set guidelines for making the decisions so that they'd make the same decisions you would in those circumstances. Set criteria for calling you or interrupting you, so that only decisions above a certain threshold of importance will come to you. Find others who can handle the problems, instead of you. Sure, it'll mean you have less control, but it'll also mean you have fewer interruptions.

• *Set hours of unavailability.* Set office hours, or hours when you must not be interrupted except for absolute emergencies. Then you can deal with problems/requests at certain times of the day, and focus during other times.

• *Delegate a backup decision*-maker. If you're a manager/owner, set up a second-in-command, so that when you're away from the office, or if you take a few hours off for uninterrupted time, problems can still be solved. Train the second-in-command so that she knows how to make the decisions appropriately.

• *Set expectations.* Staff or coworkers only interrupt you because they have the expectation that you'll respond and that it's OK to interrupt you at any time. If you change those expectations, you can channel the requests/problems to a time that you want to deal with them. For example: tell people that you only check email at 3 p.m. (or whatever works for you), because you need to focus on other work, and that they shouldn't expect a response sooner. Or tell people that you will no longer take calls or text messages after 5 p.m., but that they should email you instead and you will respond to their emails in the morning. Or whatever works for you—the point is to set a plan of action and manage the expectations of others so that you can stick to that plan.

• *Be in the moment.* If you're unable to get away from the interruptions, then learn to deal with each interruption one at a time, when possible, and give your full attention to each person, each problem, as you deal with them. This allows you to be less stressed and to deal calmly and fully with every person who needs your attention.

• *Focus when away from work.* If you can't find focus at work, because of the need to be interrupted at all times, at least find time away from work when you can clear away distractions and find time for quiet, peace, reflection, reading, writing, creating.

Bosses

What if your boss is the problem—he or she won't allow you to make the changes you need to find focus? That's a definite problem—the boss might expect you to answer texts, emails, calls immediately, to attend meetings all day long, to be busy at all times, to work long hours, to take calls after hours and do work at night . . . in short, to be inundated by interruptions at all hours.

Unfortunately, there are only so many things you can do if things aren't under your control. Here are a few ideas:

• *Talk to your boss.* Often, bosses can be very reasonable if you give them a compelling argument, and especially if you've proven yourself in the past. Sit down and talk to your boss about your desire to find focus, and explain that this will increase your productivity and creativity. Give him a copy of this book if you think it'll help (or just email the chapter specifically for managers). Ask for some specific changes, and suggest a test period of a week or two, in which you make the changes and show the results.

• *Change what's under your control.* If there are some things you can't change, then figure out what you can change, and focus on that. If you can't change your hours, at least declutter your desk and computer. If you must answer all emails at all times, at least learn to block other things on the Internet that distract you.

• *Work away from the office.* You might have the flexibility to work from home or at a coffee shop or library away from the office, or you might make a compelling argument for this change. Take this opportunity when you can, and bring a pair of earphones, turn on some peaceful music (or energizing music if you prefer), clear away distractions, and focus.

• *Prove that it works.* Make what changes you can, and show that it can bring results. Solid evidence is the best way to win over the boss.

• *Or find another job.* If your job is horrible, and your boss isn't reasonable, or the demands are too crazy and you can't possibly find the time to focus, it might be worth considering a change of jobs. That's your decision, not mine, but I changed jobs at least twice when I was unhappy with the expectations, and both times it was a very good change for me.

Unsupportive People

Another problem is that people in our lives can sometimes be unsupportive, or fat out against changes we want to make. If this person is a spouse or significant other, or someone else upon whom we depend, this can make things very difficult. Nearly impossible, sometimes.

This is actually a very common problem, and I can't give you solutions that will work in all cases. I can share some things that have worked for me, in hopes that they might help:

• *Don't force.* When we try to push others to make changes, they often resist. It's not smart to try to force other people to make the changes you want to make. Instead, try some of the tips below—setting an example, sharing, asking for help.

• *Share why it's important, and how it affects you.* Communication is important here—sit down and talk to this person (or people) about why you want to make these changes, why it's important to you, what it'll help you to do. Share the positive effects as you make the changes, and also share the problems you're facing. This type of open communication can help persuade the other person to get on board with your changes, if done in a non-pushy, non-judgmental way.

• *Enlist their help.* When you ask someone to change, they will probably resist, but when you ask them to help you change, that's much more likely to succeed. Try as best you can to make it a team effort—working together is a much better proposition than working against each other.

• *Set an example.* If the other person doesn't want to change, that's OK. Make the changes yourself, and show how great it is. If the other person is inspired by your example, that's even better. Often leading by example is the most persuasive technique there is, but don't be disappointed if the other person doesn't decide to follow your example. Be happy with the changes you've made yourself.

• *Change what you can.* If the other person is unsupportive, there might be limits to what you can change. Recognize these boundaries, and work within them.

27

Managers Transforming Office Culture

If you're an employee with little control over your schedule, there might not be too many ideas for finding focus that you can implement during your work day. In that case, I suggest you 1) implement what you can; and 2) buy a copy of this book for your manager and/or upper management, and especially point them to this chapter.

The rest of this chapter is for management: CEOs, vice presidents, supervisors, middle managers, small employers. Bosses of all kinds. Anyone who controls the schedules of others, or has influence on the policies and office culture that determine how people work.

The problem: Modern offices pride themselves on efficiency and productivity, but the truth is they are busy, hectic, overwhelming places (in general). Employees often work in cubicles that are surrounded by distractions, they are constantly interrupted by emails, IMs, texts, calls, notifications, calendar requests, people walking over to talk to them, outbursts in the office, meetings.

These distractions destroy focus. They lead to stress, to information overload. They fragment an employee's day and attention, so that it becomes an extremely bad environment for creating, for focusing on what's truly important, for producing incredible work.

Busywork isn't important work. While an employee can be busy for 10 hours a day, keeping up with all the emails and calls and meetings and nonstop requests, they might spend the day getting nothing done of any real importance. What matters is creating, is producing the next great thing that will become the cornerstone of your business, is improving the quality of your product so that the customer takes notice, is providing truly great service. Busywork isn't what matters, and yet it interrupts us and consumes all of our time and attention.

The solution: Create an environment where focus is possible.

There are many such environments, but to give you a picture of what's possible:

• The employee comes in, sits down, and figures out what matters most for today. What are the 3–5 tasks that most need to get done, that will make the most difference for the company or organization? No checking email or voicemail at this point—just quiet, and focus.

• He then sits down and, with a completely clear desk, blocks out all distractions—no phones or other mobile devices, no email, no notifications, nothing to disrupt. He works on the first task on the list.

• Later, he might go through email and voicemail and process everything that needs to be quickly processed, for 30 minutes or so.

• During the day, his focus is completely on the tasks that matter most. Very few meetings or calls interrupt these tasks.

• At the end of the day, the employee might have a short meeting with you, just to review the day, go over any problems, and perhaps agree on tomorrow's important tasks. Meetings should be held to a minimum, as they are time-consuming and can interrupt the time needed to focus on important tasks. They should also be kept as short as possible.

This is obviously just one way of creating a focused environment, but it won't work for everyone. There are lots of ideas that might help create such an environment, including but not limited to:

• Email-free Mondays: Everyone is free from email—banned from email in fact—for an entire day, and must work on something really important. Email-free afternoons or mornings are other ideas.

• Headphones: Allow employees to wear headphones to block out distractions.

• Let employees work from home one or two days a week, reporting at the end of such days what they got done. Allow them to work without the distractions of the office, and see what happens.

• Shut down the Internet for a couple hours a day. Disconnecting might seem alarming, but it will allow people to focus and get a lot done. If they know it'll happen at a certain time each day, they'll get the tasks done that require the Internet before that time, and prepare for the time of disconnection.

However you do it, creating an environment of focus rather than distraction and busywork will breathe new life into your organization.

Transforming Culture: The next question becomes how you go from the current office culture and environment to one of focus. This isn't easy—whether you don't have completely control over the company (you're a mid- or low-level manager) or you are in charge but must deal with inertia and ingrained habits.

Some ideas:

• *Give out a copy of this book.* You can freely distribute the free version of this book, which is uncopyrighted, or buy the digital package once and distribute it electronically to the rest of your organization, or buy multiple copies of the print book to hand out. It's a great place to start, to get everyone on the same page.

• *Talk about it.* Simply start a conversation, with your colleagues, bosses, team members. Talk about the problems of distractions and finding focus, and see what ideas emerge.

• *Institute small changes.* There's no need to drastically overhaul culture overnight. Start small, with a simple but powerful change, such as: instituting a no email, no meetings, no distractions period for one hour at the start of every day.

• *Keep pushing for small changes:* reducing the number of meetings, having no-email or no-Internet hours during the day, holding retreats where people work in a monk-like, distraction-free, quiet environment, encouraging people to switch off phones and use headphones during parts of their day, suggesting that people set two or three times a day when they check email and that they don't check email at other times, etc.

Over time, things can change, but be patient, be encouraging, be positive. And most of all, lead by example.

CPSIA information can be obtained at www.ICGtesting.com
Printed in the USA
BVOW032244231011

274351BV00001B/148/P